With vulnerability and hu...___.., ...m runge shares her story of spiritual growth, redemptive suffering, and her quest for healing. She does a masterful job of showing God's Grace and Mercy throughout the book. In sharing her trials and triumphs, Kelli's inspiring story offers hope and encouragement. I highly recommend you read this engaging and beautifully written book.

– Lisa Van Bramer MD, MSPH|RMRPI:
The Lepanto Project.

Roses from Heaven is an amazing testimony! Kelli's story will reach the most broken people and show them there is hope. Written in a vulnerable and moving style, this book is exceptionally hard to put down! It's full of amazing signs of God's love and intervention in order to bring a wounded woman back to Him!

– Pamela Garcia, MA LPCC

Roses from Heaven is an honest and intimate memoir that took me on a journey of joy, heartbreak, and redemption. There were multiple 'goosebump' moments as the author tells her story and shares her foreknowledge and faith. This is a book I couldn't put down!

– Katherine Rinehart, Catholic wife, and mother.

My dear friends, I strongly recommend this book. In Kelli's life accounts, you will encounter the power of the Father's forgiveness that Kelli encountered in different individuals in her life and as she opened herself up to the Father's forgiving love, she has brought that love to many different people, even people who had rejected her in different ways. For a world that needs to encounter the Father's forgiveness and always present and divine love, please read this book!

– Father Rick Nakvasil, Pastor,

All Souls Catholic Church.

ROSES FROM HEAVEN

...my story of grace and redemption

Kelli Yunge

Published by
Hybrid Global Publishing
333 E 14th Street
#3C
New York, NY 10003

Manufactured in the United States of America, or in the United Kingdom when distributed elsewhere.

Yunge, Kelli.
Roses from Heaven
    ISBN: 978-1-961757-19-6
    eBook: 978-1-961757-20-2
    LCCN: 2023920767

Cover design by: Julia Kuris
Copyediting by: Claudia Volkman
Interior design by: Suba Murugan

"if then my people, upon whom my name has been pronounced, humble themselves and pray, and seek my face and turn from their evil ways, I will hear them from heaven and pardon their sins and heal their land. Now, therefore, my eyes shall be open and my ears attentive to the prayer of this place."

2 Chronicles 7:14-15

"But if ever you turn away and forsake my commandments and statutes which I set before you, and proceed to serve other gods, and bow down to them, I will uproot the people from the land I gave and repudiate the house I have consecrated for my name. I will make it a proverb and a byword among all nations. And this house which is so exalted—every passerby shall be horrified and ask: 'Why has the Lord done such things to this land and to this house?' And the answer will come: 'Because they abandoned the Lord, the God of their ancestors, who brought them out of the land of Egypt, and they embraced other gods, bowing down to them and serving them. That is why he has brought upon them all this evil.'"

2 Chronicles 7:19-22

Dedication

This book is dedicated to my Mom and Dad, my loving parents who adopted and raised me, and to my birth mother, Mary, thank you for having the courage and strength to give me up. I love you all very much. It is also dedicated to my husband and my children—without you, my road to healing would have been much harder.

Each of you is an example of unconditional love; you all have loved me, seen me at my highest and my lowest points, and never stopped loving me or believing in me.

To all the people who encouraged and said yes to this book in any way, thank you from the bottom of my heart, and may God Bless you abundantly!

Table of Contents

Introduction

"God decided in advance to adopt us into his own family
by bringing us to himself through Jesus Christ. This is
what he wanted to do, and it gave him great pleasure."
                                                    — Ephesians 1:5, NLT

This book is the story of my journey to Christ and discovering my new identity as an adopted child of the Most High God. It's the story of how my life was miraculously transformed into recognition, forgiveness, love, and healing.

Throughout my testimony, I will frequently reference specific places where, in hindsight, there was always a common thread—a literal battle for my soul (just as there is for each and every one of us). The spiritual warfare we all experience in life is vital to recognize. We must be aware of the evil one's ability to influence our emotions, intellect, decisions, and his overall capacity to literally destroy us. Satan can lead us to self-destruction of every kind, including but not limited to suicidal thoughts, extreme bouts of confusion, anger, depression, and anxiety to a higher extent than normal in those prone to it. And the spiritual warfare only intensifies as we try to get closer and closer to Our Lord. Satan is very real and if we don't recognize this, we will fail to recognize when he is leading us astray and/or exacerbating our already challenging life problems and circumstances common to all of us.

One of the most amazing things about my journey is how it both started and ended with the Catholic Church. Never did I imagine that one day I would be able to see a thread from my birth leading back to the Catholic Church. It all started with my birth mother's request for me to be adopted into a "non-strict" Catholic family. This is a story about a journey of a soul from conception to adulthood. It shows the relentless and uncompromising pursuit and love of God for a soul that almost wasn't born, to a soul that was so sensitive and broken and often so sinful. It tells the intricate tale of an innocent baby and shows how the enemy's lies started when she was a young girl. This is the "primal wound" that many children suffer.

My journey starts with the lies of the enemy, but it ultimately ends with my identity as a chosen daughter of the Most High God. Along the way, although I experienced much pain and heartache (some of my own doing, some out of my control), with the Lord's help I literally fought to survive the perils of life and was able to triumph over my suffering, ultimately being led back to the Catholic Church where I've found refuge and safety through the sacraments.

In these pages, I will share my most painful and shameful sins, my experiences with angels and demons, my journey through adoption, the divorce of my parents as well as my own, a most painful and regretful abortion, drug and alcohol abuse that led to sexual abuses, painful marriage struggles and heartaches, and also deathbed conversions I've been privileged to witness as a hospice nurse.

Sharing my story is the very least I can do to give back to my Lord and Savior, and to be 100 percent transparent, he actually asked me to share it. At first, I was terrified. How could I share these most intimate, very painful areas of my life? Even the good things I had to share—would people even believe them? Some are still hard for me to believe myself. But ultimately, Jesus told me, "If you can help anyone avoid any of the pain and hurt you have gone through, then all your suffering will not be in vain." It has taken a lot of spiritual strength for me to let go of all human attachments and only focus on Jesus's relationship with me. He also gave me a huge gift in allowing me to experience a very personal and sweet relationship with the Most Holy Blessed Mother.

This is my battle story, but it's mostly my love story to God my Father. I'm so incredibly thankful and blessed for the way he never gave up on me; his love never ceases to amaze and astound me. God never gives up on anyone (even those we might assume are too far gone), and everyone always has the choice to repent while they are alive. God is the only one who will never fail us, never stop pursuing us, never stop forgiving us. We are all men and women of the Most High God, and he offers the gift of eternal salvation to us all.

"But a time is coming, and has come, when you will be scattered, each to his own home. You will leave me alone. Yet I am not alone, for my Father is with me. I have told you these things, so that in me you may have peace. In this world you will have trouble. But take heart! I have overcome the world." (John 16:32-33, NIV)

"Beloved, do not be surprised that a trial by fire is occurring among you, as if something strange were happening to you. But rejoice to the extent that you share in the sufferings of Christ, so that when his glory is revealed you may also rejoice exultantly. If you are insulted for the name of Christ, blessed are

you, for the Spirit of glory and God rests upon you."
(1 Peter 4:12-14)

"Then Jesus approached and said to them, 'All power in heaven and on earth has been given to me. Go, therefore, and make disciples of all nations, baptizing them in the name of the Father, and of the Son, and of the holy Spirit, teaching them to observe all that I have commanded you. And behold, I am with you always, until the end of the age." (Matthew 28:18-20)

CHAPTER 1

In the Beginning

"We know that all things work for good for those who love God, who are called according to his purpose."
—Romans 8:28

My story starts with my birth mother, Mary. She had already relinquished her first daughter, my half-sister Kristin, for adoption, and was now the single mother of two other children.

While struggling as a single mom, her parents decided to take her and my half-brother and sister to the mountains for a little getaway. She went out one night to the local college bar in Steamboat Springs, Colorado, where all the college kids hung out. She met a young man, and they ended up dancing the night away and spending the night together. The next day, she was supposed to meet up with him again, but something happened and that fell through.

She went home and eventually learned she was pregnant. She was unsure of who the father was because she had an on-again, off-again boyfriend at the time. She was actually planning to have an abortion, but her sister-in-law was a practicing Catholic and talked her out of that decision. Instead she chose to give me life, knowing the suffering she would now surely endure again for a second time.

I was born on May 3, 1975. My birth mother's mind wasn't fully made up (as far as giving me up for adoption) after giving birth to me. Her family had told her they would help her, but she didn't feel confident that it would be enough since she was already struggling as a single parent of two young children. So, after three days of holding me, breastfeeding me, and bonding with me, she named me Mary (this will be significant later on) and made the heart-wrenching decision to give me up, thinking that that was the best decision for me.

My birth mother is one of the strongest women I know. She has shared with me the details of the dark depression and suffering she endured, and I'm so thankful she was able to come out on the other end. The kind of sacrificial love she showed made my life possible, which in turn made my children's lives possible. I am forever grateful for her.

My adoptive parents were originally trying to adopt a child from the Philippines. That fell through, but then they got an unexpected call from Catholic Charities stating that a baby girl had just become available. They said they were interested and went to the agency. The way my dad told the story was quite humorous to me. I was adopted through Catholic Charities, and so when they were interviewing my parents, they asked if they were Catholic. (My birth mother had requested that I be adopted into a "non-strict" Catholic home, and they were trying to honor her request). My dad remembered replying, "Yes, we're Catholic, but we don't go to church all the time." So, there it was—my parents were found! I don't believe in coincidences; I believe that everything happens for a reason, and I believe God works all things out for the good for those who love the Lord (see Romans 8:28).

For as long as I can remember, I always felt different because I was adopted. Sometimes I thought it meant I was special, but most of the time, it meant that I was different—and in our world, unfortunately, *different* usually has a negative connotation. As a child, I was fortunate to be adopted into a large family. That made it easier therefore to blend in, and that way I didn't have to talk about being adopted very often, but it was something always in the back of my mind. It was like an annoying fly that just won't let you enjoy your picnic and keeps buzzing around you as a constant reminder of just how annoying a species can be. My parents never made me feel less special or different in any way, so I'm not sure where the negativity stemmed from.

My adoptive mom did an amazing job of making sure we were all baptized, made our First Communions and were confirmed, and I'm very thankful for this. I recently found out that I was baptized at my fraternal grandparents' home when I was two months old. I believe these sacraments were extremely instrumental in providing me with graces and protection. For anyone reading this who is not Catholic, I want you to know that the Catholic Church does consider most baptisms valid, even if not done in the Catholic Church.

I didn't learn until later in life how important these sacraments are, imparting wisdom, protection, and an inner knowing of God that would become quite instrumental in my survival during my childhood and adolescent years.

Baptism is God's most beautiful and magnificent gift…We call it gift, grace, anointing, enlightenment, garment of immortality, bath of rebirth, seal, and most precious gift. It is called gift because it is conferred on those who bring nothing of their own; grace since it is given even to the guilty; Baptism because sin is buried in the water; anointing for it is priestly and royal as are those who are anointed; enlightenment because it radiates light; clothing since it veils our shame; bath because it washes; and seal as it is our guard and the sign of God's Lordship. (*Catechism of the Catholic Church*, 1216)

My mom described the priest who performed my Baptism as "a very holy priest, a very kind man." My mom and dad received the following letter from him. I was prompted by the Holy Spirit to share it here because of the wisdom of this priest and how he so eerily seems to foretell the future in some ways. It reads as follows:

July 10, 1975

Dear Anne and Terry,

It was certainly good to see you again at the occasion of the baptism of your daughter Kelli. It was so good to gather with your families and to enjoy your presence. I hope that we will not be strangers as long as you live in Denver. It certainly is good to know that you are not living too far away.

A baptism is always something great, a sign of the future, a sign that the Body of Christ is growing. There is so much criticism in modern times about everything. No one is any longer satisfied with what exists at present.

At one time, the experience of the older generation was the guarantee of actual or desirable order. But now it is exactly that order which is attacked, precisely because it is inherited from the past. It is overturned rather than conserved and renewed, in the blind hope that what is new will be fruitful for human progress.

No further credence is now given to the stable values of faith, culture and institutions. Men look toward the future, not from a chronological viewpoint of coherence with an organic and developing tradition, but from a rebellious, surprising and indefinable viewpoint, with an almost fatalistic and messianic confidence in a radical and general renewal and in a finally free and complete happiness.

Every baptism is futuristic. It is a radical change in the child that has received the personal application of the Paschal mystery. Something new has happened and we wished often on it would be manifested later in a radical and general renewal that is so great that Kelli will live her faith to the fulness of its completement and final goal.

Trusting that you are all fine, I bless you and I remain Yours in the love of Jesus.

Signed, Father Anton Borer

Unfortunately, my parents divorced when I was three years old. This broke my heart in ways that were compounded from my original relinquishment. As Maxine Chalker, founder and executive director of Adoptions from the Heart (a private nonprofit adoption agency, and an adoptee herself), puts it:

> We all know that divorce is hard on children. It can be even harder for adopted children since the loss of a cohesive family unit amplifies many of the difficult emotions that adoptees already deal with. Many adopted children, especially as they age, struggle over whether they truly "belong" in a family. Once that family has separated, splitting into two independent households, the question of belonging only becomes more complicated.

Even as a young child, I remember feeling guilty that my parents had chosen to adopt me, because once they were divorced, they probably felt burdened by the fact that I was there. Again, my parents never said anything to make me feel this way; it was a natural by-product of a highly intuitive and ultrasensitive child. I thought, *Wow, I'm just lucky to be here. I don't deserve to be here like my siblings.* I felt as though I was one extra thing they had to take care of, and the fact of what I thought at the time was just a random event about which family I ended up with was somewhat startling to me. I would picture someone literally handing their baby over to strangers, and I couldn't believe that the person who gave birth to me felt confident doing this. My seven-year-old mind was very perplexed by this. Now, looking back, this is the first time I heard and believed the lie from the enemy. As a little girl, I obviously didn't know it was coming from the enemy, but now over many years the Lord has revealed this to me. Other things that probably didn't help me feel secure and as though I really belonged would occasionally come from my peers who at times asked, "Why did your parents adopt you? Could they not have their own children?" This type of question was a reminder of that dark cloud that I hated to feel or think about.

Research shows that adopted children seem more prone to emotional and mental health issues.[1] I believe the effects of adoption vary from person to person, and there are obviously proven arguments on "nature versus

---

1 Dr. Toussieng, quoted in Rita Dukette, "Discussion of Thoughts Regarding the Etiology of Psychological Difficulties in Adopted Children," *Child Welfare*, Vol. 41, No. 2, February 1962, pages 66-71. See also Kathleen Kingsbury, "Adoptees More Likely to Be Troubled," *Time*, May 5, 2008, https://content. time.com/time/health/article/0,8599,1737667,00.html.

nurture." Both sides are equally important and should be taken into account when raising an adopted child. When we acknowledge a child's wounds and hurt, we allow that child to grieve. And after they grieve, they have more room to grow and heal.

Counseling is a valuable option, as well as exploring open adoptions whenever possible. Whatever the outcome, if an adoptee decides to search for his or her birth parents, they ultimately must come to terms with the fact that God the Father, who gives the most perfect love, a love that does not exist on this earth, is waiting with open arms for his children to come home. It's not always possible to find all the answers we might be searching for here on this earth, but we can all support one another, even in very little ways. I remember meeting a young, adopted boy from another country who was having many emotional and behavioral problems. I shared with him that I too had been adopted. The biggest smile appeared on his face, because, right then, he knew. Our situations were not the same—his was far more traumatic—but he was reminded that he was not alone in the emotions he was experiencing. I pray that anyone who has experienced any trauma caused by their adoption or experience in the foster care system will experience the same great spiritual healing that I have.

I don't blame anyone or hold any resentment over being adopted; I'm merely acknowledging the subsequent injury to my extremely fragile heart and soul that it caused.

Before my parents' divorce, my mom had been a stay-at-home mom and my primary caregiver, and my dad had worked. I have memories of being held by both my mom and dad as an infant; I remember feeling so safe and loved. After their divorce, as is often the case, I went from being with both my parents daily to seeing my dad with my siblings every other weekend. It was so hard. I remember sensing his pain and sadness. I would have done anything to take that pain away from him, but I was just a little girl. I tried to make sure he knew how much I loved him, and I always took advantage of being right by his side as much as possible, just soaking up the safety and love that came from him—even if that meant there was going to be lots and lots of football watching involved!

Soon my mom remarried and eventually began an in-home childcare. My new stepfather was a teacher at a nearby elementary school and had two children of his own. Now my homelife consisted of many new friends and two new brothers. (There would be more, too!) It was a very busy life!

When the divorce was new, my paternal grandmother, Grandma Matthews, could see how much it was all affecting me and would look at me with a sense of sadness and concern. She would tell me how worried she was about me because of how "tenderhearted" I was. I have no doubt that she said many prayers for me. Both she and Papa made sure I felt safe and loved. There was no place that compared to the safety and protection of sleeping in between Grandma and Papa in their big bed. My grandma would always remind Papa, "Don't roll over on her—she's just a little peanut!" and we would all laugh. I knew I was safe there; it was my first taste of Heaven on earth.

I think grandparents are such blessings. They have that opportunity to provide a safe, playful space and love without all the heavy day-to-day burdens. Somehow, when we become grandparents, it's an opportunity to make everything right and perfect what you might have not gotten right with your own kids. After Papa died, I checked in with Grandma often. She was one of my greatest loves on earth, and I truly adored her. I still frequently think of her now, and sometimes I talk to her. Especially since returning to the Catholic Church, I've learned so much about how the body of Christ is alive, with those who have gone before us interceding at times on our behalf, along with all the angels and saints.

One night at Mass not too long ago, my spirit was very low, and I was struggling with some of my closest relationships. After I received the Eucharist, as I knelt and prayed with my head down and my eyes closed, I saw my Papa in my mind's eye. Just his face, like a little window from Heaven had let him peer through the veil. I heard him say, clear as day, "I see you. WE see you." I knew he meant my grandma, my dad, and others. I was completely shocked and thrilled at the same time. I was overwhelmed with the feeling of safety and by knowing there were people in heaven who knew the exact details of what I was going through—and loved and cared for me enough to make sure I knew it. I will never forget how safe and protected that made me feel on such a personal level, and it still does.

On the night Grandma Matthews passed away, I woke up around midnight with the smell of the most beautiful perfume in the air. When my dad called the next morning to let me know of her passing, I immediately asked him if she had passed around midnight, and he said yes. I told him I had awakened in the middle of the night with a strong smell of a beautiful perfume in the air. He immediately said, "Ah, she came to see you!"

CHAPTER 2

The Seed Was Planted

"My sheep hear my voice. I know them, and they follow me."

—John 10:27

Looking back now as an adult, after subsequently deciding at a young age to marry and then also divorce, I know the complexities of that decision, and I also know that Satan loves nothing more than breaking up families, because once he can wound and puncture the hearts and put a break in the family unit, he has easier access to cause subsequential wounds.

The Lord revealed to me within the past year how the devil loves to work through our trauma. He can so easily slip into the cracks and crevasses of our minds and hearts and fill them with his lies. He tells us, "You aren't worthy of any love or forgiveness, especially from God—you've messed up too much," or "You caused that—it was all your fault." And the greatest lie of all in my case was, "That pregnancy was from an unwanted act; the child will remind you of the perpetrator, and every time you look at the child, you will remember this awful experience." It's so important to be aware of the lies of the enemy. The evil one will take advantage of our wounds, hoping the pain will take root in our hearts. Once we learn to know God's voice, we won't be so easily convinced or swayed by the evil one. As Jesus says in John 10:27 (NAB), "My sheep hear my voice. I know them, and they follow me."

The Lord showed me that it was hard for the adults in my life. Everyone was doing the best they could to move on and gain traction in our new lives. Eventually, my dad remarried, and my stepmother gave birth to a new half-brother. I now had many siblings (mostly brothers) to grow up with. We spent endless hours running around outside, wrestling, and riding bikes. Hours and hours of good times and memories would be made in the days ahead. But still, especially on my birthday every year, I would remember that "monster in the closet"—that one particularly annoying situation that there was another part of me, and I didn't know anything about that, or if it even mattered, but somehow deep down I guess it did, even if I didn't want it to.

I would still have those moments at night when I would be lying in bed in the dark and suddenly look at the window and immediately a fear would come, causing me to think, *My own parents didn't even want me.* I would wonder if I had done something wrong for this to happen. Satan planted those lies and I didn't know any better than to believe him. Even though I tried to push the thoughts away, sometimes I would be horrified that maybe I was related to a "bad person," and that thought would terrify me. In my mind, if my birth parents were good, I was sad to think they didn't want me—and if they were bad, I would be terrified that they might someday come to reclaim me. Especially on my birthday, I would wonder if my birth mother ever thought about me or even remembered me.

On many of those nights, I remember seeing an angel in the corner of my room. I would look up and think nonchalantly, *There's my angel.* This comforted me, especially if I was having an episode of what I know now was "sleep paralysis." During these times, I would wake up but not be able to move a muscle—I was literally paralyzed. Other times I would sleepwalk, usually ending up next to Mom's side of the bed. I'd wake up when she would notice me and say, "It's okay—go back to bed."

I also daydreamed a lot, especially in school. I wasn't too interested in school. Recess was fun, and my friends were nice, but I was distracted a lot and had a difficult time following what was going on. I would frequent the nurse's room pretty much every week, as much as I thought I could possibly get away with. She was a very nice and kind woman, and I found it a great "time out" when I needed to escape the business of the classroom and would take refuge in the peaceful breaks I would receive there. I was stunned I never got in trouble, and honestly, I think my mom found it a little amusing. She would say, "I heard you visited your friend again today."

My mom would drop me off at CCD classes on some evenings. During one class, the teacher said there was only one sin that God couldn't forgive. Presumably she was speaking of blasphemy of the Holy Spirit. I remember immediately thinking that I must have done this at some point, and I was sure my chances for Heaven were over. I cried and cried and believed that I had somehow committed the unforgivable sin and had lost my chances at Heaven forever.

If this sounds dramatic and heavy, it was. For a young girl who was already confused about life and hurt by many things, it was just overwhelming. The CCD teacher assured me that God loved me, but I didn't believe it. I was sure I was too messed up and just not going to ever be enough for God. The enemy had been extremely successful with his first attacks on me to insure I was filled with insecurities, fear, unworthiness, distrust, and even intrusive thoughts at a young age. I didn't share these thoughts or emotions with anyone. I already thought I was just lucky to have a family that looked after me and seemed to love me—I wasn't going to burden anyone with the inner workings of my mind. But even then, unbeknownst to me, God knew and was preparing to reveal his truth to me in a mighty way. He was going to show me that this hurt, scared little girl was eventually going to be okay. She was eventually going to be able to call herself a Beloved Daughter of the Most High God, the King, the Savior, the Christ.

"Do you not know? Have you not heard? The Lord is the everlasting God, the Creator of the ends of the earth. He will not grow tired or weary, and his understanding no one can fathom. He gives strength to the weary and increases the power of the weak. Even youths grow tired and weary, and young men stumble and fall; but those who hope in the Lord will renew their strength. They will soar on wings like eagles; they will run and not grown weary, they will walk and not be faint." (Isaiah 40:28-31, NIV)

"Be sober and vigilant. Your opponent the devil is prowling around like a roaring lion looking for [someone] to devour." (1 Peter 5:8)

CHAPTER 3

The Lost Years

"He who trusts in himself is lost. He who trusts in God can do all things."

—St. Alphonsus Liguori

As I moved into my teenage years, I began experimenting with alcohol. I was so naive and had no idea how strong alcohol was. One night when I was about fourteen, I took a whisky bottle from my parents' liquor cabinet, went into our backyard, and a girlfriend and I each drank five or six small dixie cups of whisky straight. The effects were immediate, and I could hardly stand or walk back inside the house to return the whisky bottle to the liquor cabinet. My older brother was there talking with some friends, and he said, "Are you drunk?" I said no, just as I flipped backward over the couch and landed on the floor. And that was the last thing I remember until waking up the next day feeling horribly ill, which lasted for the entire next day. The worst part is everyone assumed that I had the stomach flu, so they weren't giving me the food I so desperately needed.

An addiction to alcohol soon followed. Alcohol instantly numbed the pain I carried around daily, and that was the first reprieve I'd ever had. I thought nothing of filling up water bottles up for school with orange juice and vodka or gin. The weekends centered around who I was going to hang out with and where we would get the alcohol that I was determined to have. On weekend nights, I became intoxicated to the point that I wouldn't remember any of my worries or pain.

The first boy I really liked went to another high school. He seemed to like me, too, and I was hopeful we could start dating. But he lost interest in me, and I learned from his friends that it was because I was always drunk—that's why he didn't want to date me.

As much as you'd think that might change the way I was living, it didn't. The escape from the pain I carried meant too much for me to stop drinking. I was thankful for any and every opportunity to drink.

One night I was depressed and crying in bed and somehow my mind went to God. *Was there really a God? And if there was, did he know how much I was suffering?* I remember saying out loud, "If you're really real, please show me." Instantly my room filled with a light that seemed to come out of nowhere and a sense of peace permeated my room. As crazy as it is to say it now, even though I believed God was answering my direct question, I didn't continue that prayer or conversation at all after that. I don't think I realized that he was right there, waiting for me to reach out again, but the episode stayed somewhere in the back of my mind.

I decided to be a nanny the summer between my junior and senior year of high school. Things with my stepmom had become stressful and Dad was traveling for work three weeks out of each month, so I thought it would be good to get away. My dad agreed, and I immediately called my aunt who lived in Vail, Colorado. She happened to know someone who only lived a couple blocks from her, and things got arranged very quickly. I loved being away, and I loved the mountains. In the mountains I felt peaceful, and the beauty was so breathtaking that I felt much better.

During this time, I began having chronic migraines. I would wake up daily with the most agonizing pain in my head. My aunt decided to take me to see her doctor. The doctor took one look at me and said, "Have you had any family problems?" Just like that, the floodgates opened, and she said, "You are suffering from depression." She sent us off with a prescription for a medication. When my stepmom heard that I had been diagnosed with depression, she called me and said, "What in the world would you have to be depressed about?" She had no idea the pain I carried around—and I had no desire to share any of that with her. I didn't take the medication for very long, and I don't even remember if it even helped, but just being away and out of the city in such a beautiful place helped. I only drank alcohol one time that entire summer—on the Fourth of July. When summer was over, I was sad, and then it was back to reality.

Somehow, I managed to graduate from high school with a GPA good enough to get into several decent colleges. I decided to go to Mesa State College in Grand Junction, Colorado. My dad had turned in the housing paperwork late, and the college had accepted too many students that year, so I had to live in an off-campus townhouse with two roommates, one of whom was twenty-nine years old. This was not an ideal way to start my college years or meet new friends, but there was no other option. From the beginning I was way out of my comfort zone and had no idea how to navigate things.

Looking back now, I wasn't ready for college at all. I had no idea who I was or who I wanted to be, although nursing appealed to me because ever since I was young, I'd had a special place in my heart for both the elderly and newborn babies. I instinctually knew they were the most vulnerable, and I felt an intuitive desire to protect them. One of our neighbors had an elderly mother whom I liked to visit, and one day she told me, "I think you are going to be a nurse."

But at college, a nursing professor told me how competitive the nursing program was and how you had to be "extremely good at math and science." Since I wasn't good at either, I decided I'd better pick something else. I hadn't yet developed the belief that with hard work and determination I could achieve anything I set my mind to. So, instead I signed up for communication classes, which were completely uninteresting to me.

I was so insecure about who I was in the world that I was easily led this way or that by any random event. For example, shortly after starting school, my first friend was Liza, a girl in my speech pathology class. She was from Grand Junction and still lived at home with her parents. We started hanging out, and she had some bad habits that I quickly took on. I had not formed a strong identity of my own, and time after time, I would become absorbed in other people's personalities and take on all their habits (whether good or bad) as my own.

It wasn't easy meeting friends living off campus. I wonder what would have happened if I had been living in a dorm and my roommate was someone serious about school or maybe even a Christian. Would my narrative have been different? I believe it would have, but unfortunately that's not the door that opened for me. Not long after Liza and I met, we got invited to a party by a few girls who were acquaintances of ours. A lot of the football players would be at this party, and we thought it would be a great time.

As usual, I was drinking to excess. I had been out on the patio talking to one guy that seemed nice. At some point the girls told me they were leaving for a while, but I decided to stay. However, I didn't realize that I would be the only girl left with probably ten or so guys. The events that followed would vastly change my life, and even as I write this now, I feel anxious and it's hard to breathe.

At one point, I told the guy I was hanging out with that I was going inside to use the restroom, and he followed me into the house. He waited for me outside the bathroom, which was located in one of the bedrooms. The next thing I remember was two more guys walking into the bedroom; one of them closed the door and stood in front of it. I looked at their faces—they were smiling at each other. My stomach sank. I immediately sensed something was wrong and felt scared. Later, when the girls got back, Liza said she had found me in a corner of a room in what she described as "a trance-like state." The guys involved denied being involved and told everyone, "We think she has something mixed-up in her head." While I don't remember the details of the assault (which

I have been told is normal and is a coping mechanism), I knew something bad had happened to me because I began having panic attacks within days.

I was terrified of any man—even the mailman in broad daylight. I didn't want to leave the townhome I was living in. They were football players, and if this got out, their whole futures would be at risk, and I knew this. I originally did press charges, but when my memory of those specific minutes wouldn't return coupled with the humiliation and shame I felt, I decided to drop them. They were threatening defamation charges against me, and their scare tactics worked.

My dad drove down to check on me, and when I saw him, I could tell he had been crying, and that broke my heart. In the days and weeks that followed, I would wake up in the night and feel someone's hand squeezing my throat, and I felt like I couldn't breathe. I had regular panic attacks for years to come.

One of the bad habits I would inherit from Liza was smoking marijuana. I really didn't enjoy it, and it had the effect of making me extremely paranoid and anxious. But soon I would meet my first serious boyfriend, John. We became serious within a matter of days and were inseparable. He was from another mountain town and was very into rock climbing and fishing, and I really liked hanging out with him; I felt safe with him. He was also someone who smoked pot almost daily, and I drank and smoked a lot with him and his friends.

After the incident at the party, I stopped going to classes and eventually decided to drop out. My head wasn't in the right place to be serious about school. For the next couple of years, John was my boyfriend, and I ended up moving in with his family until he finished his semester. Then we decided to move into our own place together.

I knew my parents wouldn't be supportive of the way I was choosing to live, so I didn't check in with them much during this time. John found a small apartment that was part of a two-hundred-year-old house that had been divided into three different units. We ended up moving in during the middle of the night, and as soon as he opened the door—before I even stepped inside—I felt a strong presence and said, "There's a ghost here." John assured me that everything was going to be fine, so I hesitatingly followed along.

The first night nothing happened, but the second night, one of John's friends helped us move a couch and decided to spend the night on the couch in the front room (the only room with carpet). John and I slept in sleeping bags in the bedroom on the hardwood floor. In the middle of the night, I awoke to what felt like the weight of a heavy man on top of me, and I was trying with all my strength to fight it off. I thought it had to be my boyfriend having a bad dream.

As soon as the sensation stopped, I looked over in John's direction, and he was sound asleep. I immediately started screaming and woke him up and told him to turn the light on. When he saw the look on my face and I told him what happened, he immediately became extremely uneasy and frightened, to the point that he had tears in his eyes. I told him, "I don't care if we just moved in here—if anything ever touches me again, I'm out of here." He immediately said he understood and agreed. Well, over the course of the next several months we lived there, many things would happen, but nothing ever touched me again.

For example, I had brought with me a large Children's Bible my sister had given me at some point. I have no idea why I ever took it to college or to this apartment, but I did. We would come home to find random pictures of my family members (which I kept on top of this Bible) moved into the center of the room. This happened many times. I had the strangest feeling that this presence was getting its kicks out of trying to scare me.

Another time, we came home to find that every single kitchen cabinet had been opened wide. The original kitchen in this old Victorian house was part of our apartment , so there were many cabinets, and the sight of them all wide open was very strange. The weirdest thing was opening the refrigerator one day and seeing all the contents pushed to the very edge of the shelves and arranged from tallest to shortest. It was hard to believe these things were happening, yet John didn't seem to give any of it too much attention.

The worst day, though, was when I had been home alone and taking a shower. Every time I took a shower, I would feel a breeze and the shower curtain would sway back and forth ever so slightly, but there was no window in the bathroom. On this particular day, in addition to this happening, suddenly I heard a loud crashing noise, like someone had slammed a door hard. I jumped out of the shower, put on my bathrobe, and walked slowly toward the front door, hoping no one had broken in. As I reached the front room in front of the door, there was my huge, heavy Children's Bible in the middle of the room, with the pictures and candles that had been on top of it scattered everywhere, some of them broken. I was literally shaking in horror. I innately knew that this being, whatever it was, was evil and wanted me to know it was not happy. Of all the things in the apartment it could have thrown in the middle of the room, it had chosen the Bible, and I somehow knew that was significant.

I opened the front door and knocked on the door of the older lady in the upstairs apartment. I needed some company; I was frightened. She could see from my face that something was wrong, and of course I was dripping wet in my bathrobe. She immediately said, "Kelli, what's wrong?" I stood there and just couldn't bring myself to say it, but I finally blurted out, "Um, do you believe in ghosts?"

And she said, "Sure I do—what happened?" When I told her, she just laughed and said, "Oh yes, we have noticed it, too. Sometimes our lights turn off and on, or I hear footsteps. Don't worry, it's just trying to let you know it's there."

She must be out of her mind, I thought. *Letting me know it's there?* I had experienced way more than just a flickering of the lights, but it did ease my mind a bit to know that I wasn't going crazy.

After that, I had a more acute radar for this type of activity. When we came home, I would know immediately if the presence was there in our apartment. And from that point on, I always knew if there were spirits around me. Wanting to test my awareness, I would often ask people when I could feel a presence in their homes. It never failed—every time they would answer, "Yes—how did you know?" One time they told me that the people who lived in the apartment before them had their cat thrown down the stairs and other "crazy things."

Looking back now, we were living in sin outside of marriage, and we had never talked to each other about our spiritual beliefs. John also had a pornography addiction, so there were many portals for these types of spirits to be around us. Eventually I realized that John and I were not right for each other, and I called my parents to come and get me.

Returning home, I felt very hopeless and depressed. At first, I really missed John; I had truly loved him. My heart felt completely broken and I naïvely believed I would never again love anyone this much. Once again, I went straight for the whiskey; that was the only thing I could think of that would numb the pain.

I told one of my aunts that I was feeling suicidal, and she shared the news with my mom. I don't think anyone took me very seriously, but I did my best to let them know I needed some sort of help. My plan was to drink a lot of alcohol and then leave for the mountains to confront John, certain I would surely die in an automobile accident and not make it.

Some family friends who were Catholic arranged for me to spend two nights with some nuns who lived near the cathedral in downtown Denver. After a certain number of hours of basically solitary confinement in extremely small living quarters, I felt better and was ready to go home. The nuns had probably been praying for me, and I subsequently no longer felt suicidal.

Not long after that, I met the man who would become my ex-husband. A mutual friend of ours introduced us, and we were inseparable from the beginning. He was from a large Hispanic family, and when I met his family, the love between them was palpable. It felt like what I had been missing. I loved his large family, and they were so kind to me, even letting me stay in their home when things got stressful for me. Eventually, we moved out and rented our own place.

One day I wasn't feeling quite like myself, and I had a strange feeling that I should take a pregnancy test. While driving to the local clinic, I started to talk to God. For the first time in years, I pleaded with him to let me be pregnant. I knew that I didn't care too much about myself, but I intuitively knew that I desperately needed and longed to feel like I had someone who was part of where I came from, someone I could love and care for. And when I discovered that I was, in fact, pregnant, I thanked God again and again.

Over the next couple weeks, as I shared the news with family and friends, I was shocked at the different reactions

I received. Yes, I was only twenty years old, but I was dismayed that a couple people close to me wanted me to consider abortion or adoption. Not everyone, though; Grandma Matthews, for example, immediately said, "Oh, sweetie, congratulations." None of that mattered to me, though. This was my baby, and I was determined to love him, protect him, and care for him with everything in me. I immediately quit drinking and smoking and started eating healthy foods.

We lived near the Copper Mountain ski resort, and one day, as I was walking through the resort, I saw a woman making a beeline for me. She was dressed in clothes that looked like they belonged to another time and had a worn, weathered look on her face, but something about her made me feel like she was an angel. She said, "Everything is going to be OK," while looking at me with an intenseness that made me feel a bit uneasy. Then she asked, "Can I pray for you?" A little hesitantly, I said, "OK."

I don't remember the prayer, but she repeated, "You're going to be OK." And that was it. As I walked away, I kept thinking of her presence and how it felt like she not only wasn't from around there, but also like she really wasn't just a normal human either. It felt like she had a "knowing" about the details of my situation; it felt like she might have been an angel, but I wasn't sure.

As the pregnancy progressed, there were several situations that could have caused much danger to me as well as to this baby growing inside of me. But after my encounter with this woman, I remembered to pray during these situations. It was like she had reminded me of heavenly things that were beyond our comprehension most of the time. I experienced a car accident, a snowmobile accident, and rides with hitchhikers (that was the way many people traveled back and forth from Leadville to Copper Mountain). On one van ride, it was dark, the van was full of people, and the driver seemed intoxicated. No one was wearing seatbelts. We were driving in the dead of winter on a narrow windswept highway, and I was sure we were all going to die. I'm pretty sure I was the only passenger who was sober, and I told myself to pray. I prayed for the whole way with my heart in my stomach, just begging God to keep us all safe. We made it, and I can't prove it, but I knew this was a miracle.

As the birth got closer, we made our way back to Denver and settled into an apartment. I decided to work with a nurse midwife, and as my due date drew near, they decided to induce labor. We were all at the hospital for more than thirty hours. After many, many hours of the labor going on and on, I started to get the feeling like something was wrong. It was my first time doing this of, course, and at this point it's just me, my boyfriend (we weren't married yet), and the nurse midwife in the room—who was acting all hippy-dippy, as if nothing could go wrong! The baby had been in the birth canal for several hours. I didn't know that this wasn't normal, but the nurse midwife should have! Thanks be to God, all of the sudden I had a strong intuition that something was wrong. I told the midwife, "The baby needs to get out now!

She replied, "What do you want me to do?"

I yelled, "Reach in and pull him out!" I began to push with all the strength I had left. She reached in and pulled as I pushed, and finally he was out. She screamed, "He's blue! And the cord is wrapped around him!" and then she just froze and laid him down.

I closed my eyes, fearing he was dead. I yelled, "You better save him!" His dad told me he had to pick him up and unwrap the cord himself. A few minutes later, he assured me that our baby was okay, and he brought him over so I could see him. I was still in shock. I couldn't even open my eyes for a good ten minutes. My ex-husband saved our son's life, and I will be forever grateful to him. When I finally was able to look at our baby's sweet face, I thought there had never been a more perfect, angelic-looking baby ever.

We settled into a routine, and everything was going well. Even though we were young and unmarried, I felt like a good and very protective mama bear, and his dad was right there with me; we both just loved our son to death. After a couple months I started taking birth control pills. A month later, when I went in to refill the pills, the woman at the clinic asked when my last period was. I explained that I had been breastfeeding and pregnant before that, so it had been quite some time ago. She proceeded to tell me that she wouldn't refill my prescription unless I consented to a pregnancy test. I laughed and said OK. I sat in the waiting area, and when she returned, she told me I was pregnant.

I was shocked—my son would soon have a sibling! Somehow, I knew deep down that this was meant to be. I drove home and when I asked my ex-husband to guess what I had found out that day, sure enough, he said, "You're pregnant." Somehow he knew. After the initial shock wore off, we decided we should get married.

Our wedding was simple and took place in a nondenominational church. Although we were both raised Catholic, one of my brothers had started attending a nondenominational church, and I just followed his lead. So, we married and soon had another beautiful son.

My ex-husband was working for my dad's company at the time. One day he came home and said he had been training for several days with a man named Ben. This man told my ex-husband that we needed to start reading the Bible as a family and praying together. I thought it was very strange that he would bring up God at work, and I couldn't even imagine us reading the Bible together. My ex-husband then went on to say that Ben had given him his phone number, but when he called the number, it was out of service, and when he called the office at work, they had no information on anyone named Ben. I could tell from my husband's expression and the seriousness in his voice that this had shaken him up.

He told me he thought Ben might have been an angel, and he went on to say that we needed to change our lives. During this time, we had moved in with his parents while saving money for our own home. His parents were wonderful and had plenty of room, but I remember occasionally feeling uneasy in the house. They had been told that the home had previously been occupied by Satan worshipers, and that an exorcism had been performed at some point. This didn't surprise me too much as I sometimes would get that feeling of not being alone, like the feeling I would get in the other house I lived in.

On two different occasions, I would have "supernatural" experiences. The first one happened at the beginning of our relationship. We were lying on a bed in the basement, and I asked him a question. He didn't answer me right away, but immediately I felt someone quite strongly squeeze my right arm (the arm that was farthest away from him). I immediately said, "Did you do that?"— although I already internally knew the answer because it would have been impossible for him to reach across my whole body without me noticing.

He asked, "Do what?"

I immediately yelled for him to turn on the light and then went on to explain what had happened. I remember that my arm continued to ache for several minutes as the pressure had been quite firm.

While we were living there, my husband went out one night, and I stayed in and went to bed with both the boys. My older son was lying with me in the bed, and my younger son was in a small crib at the foot of the bed. Suddenly, I got a strange, uneasy feeling and decided to pray for our protection, and just as I started to pray, I heard in my left ear the loudest and scariest voice I had ever heard saying, "You think you can f-ing protect those boys?" It was a snarly, raspy, horrid voice—it was an audible voice, what I imagined a demon might sound like. I was instantly paralyzed with fear. All I could do was to say the name of Jesus over and over. Eventually, I fell asleep, and we were all kept safe despite the demon's attempt to scare me to death.

We did not go on to become prayer warriors or Bible readers at that time, but many seeds were planted, and two of the most amazing human beings were born into the world that would change us both (and many others) for the better, forever. Eventually, my ex-husband and I started having some difficulties, and when I spoke to someone whom I loved and trusted, they gave me advice that pushed me to end the marriage.

I regret that my ex-husband and I didn't turn to God right then; I wish I had taken everything to prayer and waited for God's direction. But we obviously make many, many decisions when we are living in the world and not asking God for advice about major life decisions. Although this was not where I was at this time, looking back now, God was sending a lot of heavenly protection my way.

I had no idea what was about to come, and thank God for that, because I wouldn't have had the strength to bear it all if I'd known. God knew, though, and he was there every step of the way—I just didn't know it at the time. You'll see.

CHAPTER 4

The Call

"Nowhere other than looking at himself in the mirror of the Cross can man better understand how much he is worth."

—St. Anthony of Padua

I searched for answers regarding my adoption when I was around twenty-three years old—around the same time my divorce was finalized. I found my birth mother through Catholic Charities. I attended a program called Adoptees in Search in Denver, and at these meetings, I met birth parents searching for their relinquished children and others like me looking for answers. Ultimately, I paid a small fee for an attorney to contact my birth mother, and if she was open to a meeting, the attorney would set it up. My birth mom agreed to meet, and that was amazing.

I remember the very first words she ever said to me: "I have prayed for you every single day, and I love you so much!" I couldn't help but think that this reunion was just as much for her as it was for me. She admitted that now that both of her daughters had found her and she knew we were OK, she could finally let herself heal all the way. It has been a journey of healing for both of us, as well as finding out lots of genetic predispositions and health issues that are very useful to know.

The first time I went to meet her in person, I was hoping that all the years of seeing myself in the mirror and never seeing anyone who looked similar to me was about to end. As I pulled up in front of her house (the house she had lived in since being pregnant with me), I was more nervous than excited. I might have even had some doubts about whether this was a good idea. I yearned for answers and wanted to fill the void of the unknown, but I was scared. As I parked across the street in front of her house, I saw her coming to meet me. She walked fast toward me and just hugged me with everything she had. I could tell this was such an emotional moment for her, but I was shocked at the realization that I did not have an instantaneous love or even a feeling of familiarity for this person. She was my birth mother, but she wasn't my mom who had raised me and planned birthday parties for me and taken care of me when I was sick. She was still mostly a stranger to me.

We went inside and sat on her couch, and I remember being so overwhelmed. Her feelings were so raw, so real, but I was in a whole other headspace. She begged me to forgive her, and I was perplexed by this. I didn't feel like I had held anything against her. I believed that she did what she thought was best for me, but the guilt she seemed to carry was immense. I felt bad for her, and I assured her I was fine.

I asked her if I looked like my birth father, and she started to cry. She explained that she couldn't remember a lot of details about him—only that he was tall. I was disappointed because this meant I would not meet a family member whom I resembled after all. My birth mother had darker skin than I did; she was shorter, with very thin hair and green eyes—all opposite characteristics of mine.

Since then, I have learned many details about her personality and mental health struggles as well as her huge heart for other people. Overall, meeting her was an amazing experience, and it meant the world to me how much she cared for my well-being and wanted me to be happy and healthy. I had filled a big piece of the puzzle of the unknown. I also learned about and met three new siblings, whom I have cherished getting to know, and I've seen some similarities with certain physical characteristics as well as some personality traits. My birth mother and these siblings have told me more about her life over the years. I learned that she spent many years suffering with mental health issues and substance abuse. She spent twelve days in a psychiatric facility where she recalled that a nurse spoke to her about Jesus and how eventually prayer helped her come out of that darkness. Talking with me over the years at times was very difficult for her, as it brought up the trauma that she had to live through during those years when she was pregnant as an unwed mother. During those times, unwed mothers endured extreme judgments, ridicule, and hard times. It wasn't uncommon for a woman to be sent away and hidden so as not to bring shame on the family. She carried much deep shame and guilt along with tremendous grief. I cannot even imagine what she went through, and I could never thank her enough.

My birth mom has become someone I can turn to in times of great darkness. Sometimes it made things much worse, like the time she said, "Oh honey, I'm so sorry; many of my friends are suffering right now too because Venus is in retrograde." Or when she told me she had taken half of a Lexapro to jump-start herself. Other times, especially since my conversion to the Catholic Church, she remembers her strong Catholic upbringing and is able to relate to how Jesus has saved me and revealed so much to me.

As I started my journey as a single mom of two young boys, looking back now, I can see how the Lord carried us in so many ways. Some storms were about to unfold, and I had no idea what was coming. Unfortunately, every other weekend when the boys were with their dad, I continued to drink to excess, always with the intention of just having a good time. Many times, I would end up spending the night with a stranger. Because my self-esteem was so low, I felt validated when I was getting attention from guys. It was the way I measured my self-esteem. I wish I had known much sooner that my beauty and worth came from my Heavenly Father when I was younger, but today part of my story is telling young girls where their worth comes from.

One night I attended a wedding in the mountains. I was drinking, and someone made sure I didn't have my car keys. Late that night, something upset me, and I became emotional. I decided to leave and somehow found my car keys. As I drove down the curvy, narrow mountain road, it seemed as if my steering wheel was turning on its own—I knew I wasn't in control of it. I was acutely aware that someone else (who I could only imagine was my guardian angel) was escorting me home. This was the first of two times that I was escorted home by an angel.

This kind of thing left me with an incredible heaviness that's hard to explain. My life has been spared several times, and the guilt comes from not understanding how a

God who had every right to punish me or let me succumb to my bad choices . . . for some reason didn't. I know I won't fully understand it until I get to heaven. The only thing that makes some sense to me is that God knew how much I loved him, and he knew I would try my hardest to save others and share how he saved me from so much—especially from myself.

June 15, 2022

Tonight, meditating on my past sins, I heard the Lord say, "The more wounds you have, the more access Satan has to you." In his Great Mercy, out of his love for me, God saved me, knowing that until I was fully healed, I wasn't 100 percent in my "right mind," so to speak. He said, "Yes, you knew right from wrong, but there were so many physical, spiritual, and mental healings that needed to occur." His love for us is immense, immeasurable.

I'm forever grateful and want to do whatever I can for you, Lord. Please continue to help me die to myself and offer up my sufferings. Over the past few weeks, you've revealed to me so much. Even in the conversation with Father N. How great is your love, and how much I don't deserve it! And you've even given me Mama! I love you!

My mom had been a hospice volunteer for many years, and one day, years ago, had taken me with her. I remember feeling a sense of awe and reverence, which at the time I didn't really understand. I just knew without a doubt that it was a great honor and privilege to be with someone at the time of their death. It was sacred, and God had revealed this to me. Now that I was a little older, I felt more secure about attending college, and I decided to sign up for nursing prerequisite classes.

During this time, the boys and I were settled in low-income housing for women and children. I had the best two boys ever, and that helped motivate me to get going with school. It was exciting and scary at the same time. I juggled signing up for classes, finding the best pre-school/childcare, and making sure my kids' meals and laundry were taken care of. I ran purely on adrenaline a lot of the time. It was extremely important to me that the boys felt safe and knew how much they were loved. And between time with their dad and all their grandparents and aunts and uncles, they were very loved.

When I was almost done with my prerequisites classes, I got a work/study job in the counseling and advising office at Colorado Community College. I had planned to apply to other universities and hadn't investigated the nursing program at the community college at all. But after meeting with an admissions counselor at Colorado University's nursing program, I realized I was just one point away from admission. He advised me to check the box stating I was Hispanic. I said, "Oh, no, that's my ex-husband's last name," and he said, "Well, you get an extra point if you check that box." I felt defeated and upset. If I chose to lie, apparently, I would get accepted into the school. I was a bit disappointed, especially because, truth be told, I didn't know what my heritage was since I had been adopted. But eventually I decided to join the long wait list at The Community College of Denver.

But then, when I called to make sure they had received all my required paperwork and transcripts so I could be on the waiting list, they put me on hold. A minute later, a woman came back on the line and asked, "Are you calling to accept your spot?"

I explained that I was calling to make sure I was on the waiting list. She said, "You're not on the wait list anymore—we've had your information and you're on the top of the list. We are ready for you to start if you are accepting your spot."

I was shocked, and I knew this was my sign that this was the right school and the right path. Before long, I officially started nursing school.

CHAPTER 5

Introduced to Jesus

"The one who calls you is faithful, and he will do it."
—1 Thessalonians 5: 24, NIV

I had met a married mom of several young children one day when I had taken the boys to a park to play. We exchanged numbers and became friends. At some point, she mentioned that some people had knocked on her door and shared the Gospel with her. She said they did group dating among the single people in their congregation, and she suggested that I give them a call.

I did and soon met a wonderful group of single young Christian adults. I instantly fell in love with all of them—the way they boldly prayed and openly spoke of Jesus resonated with me on a level I had never known being raised Catholic. Somehow I had missed the part about having a personal relationship with Jesus.

I immediately agreed to be baptized into the Church of Christ. They were surprised at how eager I was and asked me if I needed more time to pray about everything first. I said that I didn't. Something deep inside me felt like this was the missing piece of the puzzle. I thought, *This is what I've been missing!* I immediately started praying and reading the Bible regularly, and God didn't waste a second of time. I can remember like it was yesterday the childlike faith I had. I took every promise the Lord gave and believed every Scripture I read in the pages of my Bible.

The very first Scripture I read the Lord brought to my attention by having the words illuminate from the page as if they were floating in the air:

"Be joyful always; pray continually; give thanks in ALL circumstances, for this is God's will for you in Christ Jesus. Do not put out the spirit's fire; do not treat prophecies with contempt. Test everything, hold onto the good. Avoid every kind of evil. May God himself, the God of peace sanctify you through and through. May your whole spirit, soul, and body be kept blameless at the coming of our Lord Jesus Christ. The one who calls you is faithful, and he will do it." (1 Thessalonians 5:16-24, NIV)

I would often come back to these verses, especially meditating on the fact that it didn't say to "pray when things aren't going well"—it very specifically said to pray continually. From that day forward, oh boy, did my conversations with the Lord start! I just loved praying for everything and for anyone. I immediately felt the Holy Spirit's presence, and the Lord would bring so many things to my attention.

Sometimes it was overwhelming. If I heard people arguing or saw someone who looked upset, especially children, I would feel compelled to pray for them. If I heard about any sort of injustice, my spirit would be quick to do something. Occasionally, the Lord would tell me specific things to do, and I would do them. For instance, he would ask me to invite someone to church; other times he would protect me from something.

I was very happy attending church there and the boys seemed to like it—although I had a Catholic family member tell me it was a "cult." I wasn't sure what a cult was, but I knew how much these Christians loved God and took care of one another. They made me feel extremely special and loved. I went on dates with several of the guys (in groups), and they always seemed genuine and nice.

At the same time, it started to get to me when certain members would say, "We are the one true church." It didn't seem reasonable to me that there could be only one true church, and eventually that bothered me enough to start to miss attending some Sundays. I began to notice a weird pattern. When I skipped church, I felt like a heavy weight had been lifted off my shoulders, but when I returned, the heaviness would come back. Almost instantaneously it made sense to me: *Satan doesn't want me going.*

This affected my praying and reading my Bible as well, and I'm ashamed to say that sometimes the heaviness was just too much. Eventually, the combination of struggling with believing this group was the one true church and the heaviness of it all led me to fall away. I never completely stopped reading my Bible, and I still prayed a lot. I prayed continuously for my boys' protection, especially when they weren't with me, such as when I dropped them off at school. There was nothing that mattered more to me than my boys safety and well-being.

During this time, I had a school friend named Joy who I had several classes with. She was from Maui, Hawaii, born and raised and wanted me to come visit her and her brother Dominic in Hawaii during this time. I had a hard time leaving the boys, but I knew they would have an amazing time with their grandma and obviously I wouldn't need to worry about them, so I decided to go. During the trip, as beautiful as I remember it being, I noticed I seemed kind of down. I already missed my boys, and I didn't have the same feelings for Dominic that he had for me, so that made it kind of hard. One night, as I was asleep in one of the spare bedrooms, I was woken up and saw a small Hawaiian boy was standing inches away from the bed. He had to of been around five or six years old. I was terrified, I had often felt the presence of spirits (good and bad) but had never seen a ghost in complete form and detail before this. I jumped up and ran into the hallway, all the lights were out in the house, and I could barely find the doorknob on the door of the room next to me where my friend Dominic was asleep. When I finally found the doorknob, it was locked. I began banging on his door waiting for him to let me in. When he finally made it to the door and opened it, I yelled, "why did you lock the door!?" He said, "I didn't lock the door, I never lock the door!" He then when on to tell me that his sister had told him before that all sorts of weird things had happened in that room. I informed him I would now be staying in his room for the remainder of the trip. I couldn't wait to get home. Soon after getting home, the boys and I experienced a scary situation one day on the way to school.

We were getting ready to cross Colfax Street in downtown Denver, I would park my car a couple blocks away, walk them to school, and then attend classes. At the busy intersection, I pushed the walk button and waited for the walk sign. We were all holding hands and when we were already almost halfway across the street, I suddenly heard someone yell loudly, "STOP!" I yelled for my boys to also stop. Literally seconds after we stopped, an elderly lady ran the red light, going at least seventy to eighty miles per hour. It happened so fast! I will never forget the image of that car speeding by us driven by an elderly lady with curlers in her hair. When it was safe, we ran across the street, where we all collapsed on a nearby patch of grass.

If the person had not yelled stop, I knew that one, or possible both of my babies would have been killed instantly. I cried and held them so tight; I told them how much I loved them and how God had used that person behind us to protect us. The fact that anyone would have been looking in that direction at that exact time, with enough time to yell stop, and for me to hear it was a miracle.

I thanked God continually for his protection, and this miracle just increased my faith even more. You might think this is the point when everything clicks and I stay close to the Lord and have smooth sailing going forward, but unfortunately, that's not what happened.

CHAPTER 6

The Enemy Lurks

*"The storms that are raging around you will turn out to
be for God's glory, your own merit, and the good of many
souls."*

—Saint Pio of Pietrelcina

One night I made the decision to go out to a bar with
a neighbor I barely knew. When we arrived at the bar,
a couple of male friends of hers were there. We were
hanging out, having fun, and then toward the end of the
night, we all drove back to our apartment together. Of
course, the usual suspects of overdrinking and the stupid
decisions that often accompany it were there. When we
arrived home, I started to feel that these two guys (her
friends) assumed that I was thinking something more
would happen.

After trying to avoid these guys by going into my
neighbor's bathroom and locking the door, my neighbor
told me they were in the hallway and weren't leaving, and
that it was my fault because I had flirted with them. So,

being scared and under the influence of alcohol I ventured out into the hallway where they were.

I thought to myself, *Surely, they won't try anything with me, they know my neighbor is right across the hall.* Well, I was wrong. They didn't care and were sneaky and made themselves appear innocent and harmless as they made up a reason for needing a brief moment in my apartment.

Immediately I went into shock, as they were acting like they owned the place and could do whatever they wanted. My mind, I believe, went into shock (I obviously had a previous trauma like this situation). When a person senses danger, they either fight, flight, or freeze, and according to *Medical News Today*, this decision "is an involuntary reaction to a perceived threat that causes physiological changes" and you have very little control of how you react in a "perceived or actual dangerous situation."[2] Well, I definitely froze, at first.

Although I was initially in shock and they had succeeded for a brief time, thank God I was able to reach down deep inside of me with a strength that could of only came from God himself. With a sudden surge of anger, rage, and strength that I didn't know was there, I was able to

2 Mary West, "What Is the Fight, Flight, or Freeze Response?", *Medical News Today*, July 29, 2021, https://www.medicalnewstoday.com/articles/fight-flight-or-freeze-response.

run away and make it extremely obvious that this was no longer going to happen.

As I stood with my door open and stared them down waiting for them to leave, I guess I knew it could go one of two ways—either they doubled down and would physically fight me and I could get hurt, or the brief moment of braveness and strength that I believe God provided would pay off and they would leave—and leave they did. I realized in that moment I had somehow finally found the strength I so desperately needed and never knew I had. I've always felt guilty for these situations and blamed myself. If I had been more responsible or had not had so much to drink, I would have avoided something like this.

I told myself the next day (after going to the hospital and receiving the "morning after" pill) that this never happened. I told myself, *This is not something you will be sad or mad about—you don't have the time for counseling or entertaining anymore trauma.* And that was that. I chose to stuff this down along with all the other uncomfortable or hurtful things I had no time for.

Several weeks later, though, I learned I was pregnant. Not only was I pregnant, but I also had been intimate during this time period with someone I really loved and cared about, and now I didn't know with whom I had become pregnant. I made an appointment to see a doctor right away. I told him the entire situation, and he looked at a little calendar and then told me I had become pregnant on the night I had decided to forget. The night I decided out of fear. I thought, *There is just no way this is happening*. I had a hard time believing the Plan B pill hadn't worked, because I had taken it so soon after.

Recently, I've found out that there is a real possibility that the doctor lied to me that day. I contacted him last year and told him I needed to know if there was any possible way he could have lied to me, thinking he was helping me (knowing I was going to choose abortion if it happened the way he stated). I shared that I was seeking healing from my abortion and wanted to be sure it happened exactly the way he said it happened. (Because over the years, I kept feeling doubts and confusion and had an odd feeling that he had lied to me.) His response was, "Which answer would make it easier for you to heal and move on?"

I said, "Neither! I regret the abortion either way and deeply regret that decision." So, I'll never know whether he lied to me or not. And yes, it did cause me to subsequently choose abortion (because at that time I still believed that if a woman became pregnant against her will, she had the right to an abortion). I know now that this was just another lie from the enemy.

To make matters worse, during this time, I was briefly arrested (the details no longer matter, and I will keep private) but I learned firsthand that a person can be arrested before guilt or innocence can be established, and usually, if we are very honest, it fits into the grey area somewhere.

As hard and scary as this situation was—adding a little more PTSD for me to carry for years, along with extreme anxiety/panic attacks, I had now lost my trust for police officers I had always trusted.

It couldn't get any worse, could it? My babies weren't with me, and the only thing in the world I cared about was getting back to them as soon as possible. (A little advice here: If you ever get arrested, try not to cry because in "jail language," this means that you're apparently suicidal. And this subsequently means that you need to undress in front of four or five women staring at you, and you have to wear a heavy and filthy smock so you can't kill yourself. So don't cry.)

The next day, I started crying again as I was being escorted into an elevator with several other inmates. A tall young Black man standing about twelve feet behind me yelled, "Hey! You're going to be OK!" The prison guards immediately yelled at him for speaking to me. He didn't care, though; he saw my spirit and my broken heart, and he repeated what he said even louder as he looked intensely into my eyes. I felt like he was transferring some of his strength, along with a spiritual hug, to me. I will never forget in that moment, that at one of the lowest points of my life, God got a message to me through one of his warriors. Jail is one of the darkest, most horrible places, where the vulnerable often get preyed on. This man gave me enough strength to get through the rest of my hours there until my dad bailed me out.

Eventually I found some amazing student lawyers, and the charges were immediately reduced as they gathered more details of what had transpired. I just told the truth and decided to take the plea deal they offered me. No way was I going to put my fate in the hands of a jury—I would rather plead guilty and have probation. I trusted that the Lord would walk with me through this and would eventually make sure my records were sealed, because HE makes the final decision, not man. Later, down the road, the Lord would use this experience to give me compassion, love, and kindness when I worked as a jail nurse, but more about this later.

Unfortunately, once I was on probation, I now had a compound trauma experience that would follow me like a ghost everywhere. I wish I could go back and say this is the part where I felt secure and strong, knew this pregnancy was a blessing, decided to postpone school for a couple years, and let the Lord continue to take care of us. But the truth is, I was more scared than ever.

I decided to go through with the abortion. I was only OK with this if it was done as soon as possible. I believed what most people do—that in the first six to eight weeks, it was barely there. But when I called to schedule the abortion, they made me wait a couple weeks because of how early I was. I was furious. To me, each day that went by meant that the abortion was worse than the day before. The Lord would later reveal to me how wrong I was.

A family member gave me a ride to the appointment. Since no one in my family had said, "We are here for you if you want to have this baby," I assumed they thought I was making the right decision, but honestly, I don't know how many of them even knew. No one pressured me to have an abortion, however—it was a choice I made, and looking back now, it was completely a fear-based decision.

When we got closer to the abortion clinic, I just remember not letting myself feel anything. There was no pre-abortion explanation of what I would be going through, although I'm sure I must have signed something. No one asked if I was sure or whether I would have changed my mind if I had support. I felt very judged by a family member. (Looking back now, I realize by this family member staying neutral, it was actually their way of supporting me, they couldn't read my mind, and they didn't know how much I was dreading this and how overwhelmed I was.) And afterward, I saw how this had affected them deeply too.

As they walked me back and I sat on the table, there was a doctor and a nurse, I assume. I remember crying in front of the doctor, an older man, and he was so kind. He said, "Everyone makes mistakes, and they can pretend like they are perfect, but they aren't." By his kind and sensitive manner, he gave me a false sense of security. He was a doctor, and I looked up to most medical professionals at that time. I believe this doctor genuinely from his heart of hearts felt like he was doing a kind and compassionate thing for me. There was no part of me that sensed that he was doing it for the money or because he really loved the job. I knew in my heart that he cared and wanted to help me, and he believed that he helped me that day, and for some time I guess I did too.

I must forgive myself; maybe I have, although I'm not sure how I could. The emotions run back into my mind, all the what if's. The wondering that if the nurse hadn't forcefully grabbed my arm and injected me with an unknown substance, could I have changed my mind? Whatever it was, it worked because the next thing I remember was probably just moments later when the medication must have worn off and the doctor had to tell me, "Hold on a few more seconds; it's almost done." I was awake and in absolute horror that this was really happening, and I couldn't even imagine what was going on and tried to just shut my mind off and just pray for it to be over.

I remember when it was over and I was back at my apartment, I felt so alone. I vividly remember just sitting down at the kitchen table and suddenly having this overwhelming sense of a presence in the room with me, and that's when it hit me: "Oh my gosh, I just had an abortion; I just killed my baby." I stood up and walked over to the kitchen sink to get some water, and I will never forget the switch on the coffeepot turning on by itself; within seconds I had an overwhelming sense that I wasn't alone. Then, seconds later, I had a real sense of feeling alone and empty and wondering where my baby was now. Suddenly, it wasn't just this "problem" or "inconvenience."

Now, suddenly, the reality of knowing it was a baby left me in absolute shock. On the way to the abortion clinic, it was a "barely there clump of cells" and now, it was a baby?! I believe many women probably do what

I had done; the fear and overwhelming pressure of the situation we feel is too much for us to bear. (What we don't realize at the time is that we are completely shutting ourselves down and not letting ourselves feel—it's a way of coping with such a difficult, stressful situation.) We are told that abortion is healthcare; it's a medical necessity; it's a woman's right to choose. These are all lies. It's the absolute murder of the most innocent and vulnerable in our society.

If it is legitimate healthcare, why aren't there follow-up appointments after abortion procedures? Why don't they tell you before your procedure that some women die during or following abortions? Why don't they tell you about the very real post-traumatic stress conditions following abortion procedures, or that many women will be put on antidepressants or other psychotropic medications? My abortion added much more trauma for me to carry around, but I stuffed it down as far as I could; it was obviously much too uncomfortable to let myself be reminded of daily. The only stark reminder that I could not control was the date of April 7th. This was said to be the due date for my baby, so every year I dreaded that day like the plague and would just continue to push it out of my mind, as deep down as I could. Because somehow, I knew that that kind of pain, the pain of realizing you let someone kill your growing child, no matter how the pregnancy came to be, was not a pain you could feel every day and be okay. Unbeknownst to me—but known to Almighty God—this was something I would need much healing from. And he was ready to lead me when the time was right.

CHAPTER 7

On Shaky Ground

"For the word of the cross, to them indeed that perish, is foolishness; but to them that are saved, that is, to us, it is the power of God."

—(1 Corinthians 1:18)

Years later I met and married my husband, Hans, after we met in nursing school. We were inseparable from the start, and he quickly became my best friend and closest confidant. We decided to get married after only five months of dating. I deeply yearned to have another baby and desired for my boys to get to have another sibling. Three weeks after we got married, we found out we were expecting a baby.

This was one of the first times the Lord was able to show me so vividly that life begins at conception. My husband and I both knew I was pregnant; we both witnessed the room being illuminated with a light and an angelic presence. This was the first sign of many when the Lord showed me that HE is the author of life and that it begins at conception. Before I knew it, another angel had joined us in the form of a new precious baby boy. We named him Noah, which means "repose" or "rest." His presence brought such great tranquility to all our hearts, and his brothers loved him from the start.

Hans and I began our marriage with the greatest of intentions and love, but unfortunately, when two people with many unhealed wounds come into a relationship, a spiritual battle is sure to ensue. Sister Lucia of Fatima told Cardinal Carlo Caffarra that a "decisive battle between the kingdom of Christ and Satan will be over marriage and the family."[3] My husband and I have felt this "battle" in our marriage from the very beginning. We literally felt spiritual warfare so often that it seemed we seldom got any reprieve from it.

Marriage is hard enough when two people who are healthy and healed come together, but we were both immature and not well formed in many ways. We would go through many ups and downs, including infidelity, separations, insecurities, as well as making many good memories. It was nice to have someone I felt so comfortable with and being able to share and really understand each

3 Philip Kosloski, "Fatima Visionary Said Final Battle Would Be Over Marriage and Family," May 13, 2022, *Aleteia*, https://aleteia.org/2022/05/13/fatima-visionary-said-final-battle-would-be-over-marriage-and-family.

other's work stressors, since both of us being nurses was very bonding. But even through the separations, the Lord was holding me in his hands. For example, once when we were separated for a short time, in a way, I could say that I felt my faith increase. He showed me that he has a special place in his heart for widows and orphans, single moms, etc. During this time, I had a prayerful conversation with Our Lord about tithing. I wanted to do and give whatever he would have me give, but I wasn't sure how much I could afford or what would be responsible. I heard the Lord say, "Keep some money in your wallet, and when you see an opportunity to give to someone in need, offer them the money." I thought it was very sweet that he gave me a precise plan. I made sure over the next few months to always keep some money in my wallet, and I can tell you that people seemed to be coming "out of the woodwork"! A few times a week random people would cross my path or my car would end up stopping right next to a homeless man.

This period gave me such joy and comfort during this time, because I knew the Lord saw me, heard me, and was intimate in my life and had a personal relationship with me through the Holy Spirit and his promptings. One day, a homeless man approached me, but I didn't have any money available in my wallet. I told the man, "I'm so sorry, I don't have any money with me." Within seconds and without hesitation he said, "It's okay—there's an ATM right down there!" I was a little surprised at his boldness and forwardness, but I had to chuckle, and in my mind, this was part of the whole divine leading by the Lord. It provided my heart with a wonderful distraction during this time that the Lord knew I desperately needed.

Another day, my sons and I were on our way to Colorado Community Church, a non-denominational church we'd been attending. I suddenly remembered I had given my last five dollars the day before to a homeless man on the corner. I told the boys, "If I stop at an ATM, we will be late to church, but if we don't, I won't have money to give." Immediately my middle son said, "Mom, you have money in your wallet—it's right here!" I reminded him I had given away my last five dollars the day before. He kept saying, "The money is right here."

Then he said, "It's eighty dollars."

"Well then," I said, "that's a miracle—because I know I didn't have that money!"

Within seconds the Lord told me in the silence of my soul, "Give this much money to the church, give this much money to a random person that I will show you, and with the leftover money, buy your boys lunch." I was shocked and surprised by the specific details. I was nervous, too, because I had a strange feeling that he didn't mean a homeless person on the way to church; he meant someone *in* the church. *How could I give money to someone at the church?* I didn't want to make anyone uncomfortable, and I thought that they might think I was somehow better than them if I had money and knew they needed it.

When we arrived at church, we were seated in an overflow room with round tables. During the sermon, my eyes immediately went to a young woman sitting at the table I was facing, and I felt my heart drop. Immediately, the Lord said, "She's the one." I tried to ignore him; I felt uncomfortable. *How can you ask me to do this here, Lord, in front of so many people?* I don't know what all the anxiety was about—just the task at hand, perhaps, or having second thoughts and worrying that maybe I heard him wrong.

As the service came to a close and everyone slowly got up and moving, I looked at my two sons who were sitting on a little bench sort of facing the table with the girl. I asked them to look over and described to them what the girl looked like. After they spotted her, I said, "The Lord asked me to give her this money," (holding it in my hand). I decided a quick trip to the bathroom was needed. As I tried to stall in the bathroom, I heard the Lord say, "Hurry up, she's going to leave," and then with a tad more serious tone, "I asked you to do this; give her the money." I begrudgingly left the bathroom, and with my heart racing, I spotted her. At some point I even asked my boys if they would give her the money, but their response was immediate and sharp: "No, *you* give it to her!"

As I walked up to her, she gave me a huge smile. We said hello, and then I said, "Listen, when we were driving to church today . . . long story . . . I didn't have money in my wallet, and then some miraculously appeared . . . and the Lord told me to give you some of the money. It's not mine: it's from the Lord."

She seemed shocked and insisted that she couldn't take the money. With everything in me, I begged, "Please take the money. It's not my money; it's from the Lord, and he wants you to have it. Please, please, just take it!"

She reached out to hug me, and then she whispered in my ear, "You will never know how much I needed this money!"

I couldn't believe it! The Lord had done it again! I only wished in that minute that I had had more to give her, but the smile on her face carried me through many days with absolute joy that the Lord was with me and close to me, and there was nothing that I wanted more than that.

A few weeks later, I somehow misplaced my wallet, and it had some receipts in it that I really needed. Immediately

I remembered the Lord promises that "with faith as big as a mustard seed you can move mountains." I decided that asking the Lord to have my wallet miraculously appear wasn't too much to ask. It was an unnecessary burden, and my day-to-day stresses during this time were enough on their own. So I prayed, "Lord, you said that with the faith of a mustard seed we can move mountains. Well, I'm not asking for a mountain to move—I only need my wallet to appear. I don't care where it is—whether someone stole it or it was left on top of my car and I drove off. You are God, and there is NOTHING you cannot do, so surely with as much faith as I have (I was sure it was more than a mustard seed), you will have my wallet show up."

I don't know what got into me, as ridiculous as it sounds, but over the course of the next two weeks I told several people that my wallet had disappeared, but I was sure the Lord was going to have it appear. Each day I would keep praying as fervently as I could and wouldn't allow any doubt to creep in.

During this time, I had scoured the apartment, my car, emptied out my work bag (literally dumping the entire contents onto the floor multiple times). Then, one morning, I was alone and talking on the phone with a friend. As I ended the conversation, as ridiculous as it sounds, my last statement to her was, "I know the wallet is going to show up." As I hung up the phone and turned toward my work bag, there was my wallet sitting on the very top of the bag, just clear as day. I couldn't believe my eyes! I screamed and jumped up and down as I thanked the Lord for the gift of this answered prayer.

These instances always amplified my faith and drew me closer to the Lord. The last instance that comes to mind during this time was what I now realize was my first encounter up close with a demon-possessed man. I saw a man rummaging through a dumpster, and I had money on me, so I went straight toward him, hoping to help so he didn't have to do that. As he turned around, I saw that his eyes were so very dark. I remember thinking that something was very wrong, that he was filled with rage and anger. I instantly felt he was demon-possessed, and I wasn't sure what to do. I was scared and wanted to drive away, but I had already reached out my hand with money. He hesitated and didn't take the money for what seemed like a really long time, and then, just as I was about to pull my arm back in the car and drive away, he snatched the money from my hand. It was extremely scary.

As much as the good signs like this from God were encouraging, there were plenty like this that brought me back down to reality that demons and angels really exist, and they both dwell among us all the time. They are present whether we are aware of them or not, whether we choose to believe it or not.

Just recently, I was in downtown Denver at a salon. As I came into the main waiting area, I saw a young woman walking in circles with her head tilted back. In my spirit immediately I knew she had a demon, and I felt immediate fear and anxiety as I also had a strong feeling that she was going to approach me, and I wasn't prepared for that. I immediately went back to the bathroom and took refuge for five or ten minutes until I was sure she would be gone. After a few minutes, I walked toward the front again and opened the door to the lobby. I saw in my peripheral vision that one of the salon employees had approached her and politely explained she was welcome to come back anytime she had an appointment, but that their policy didn't allow people to otherwise hang out there. She got up and left quickly.

After I checked out and walked to my car, I felt guilty and thought maybe I had misinterpreted the situation. But I knew if my instincts were right and she was going to approach me like I felt, I was definitely not someone who was equipped to help or deal with that situation unfortunately (more than to just pray for her, of course). I started praying as I started to drive home out of the city, because if I had been wrong, I wanted the Lord to let me know. As I pulled up to a stoplight, I looked out the window and saw a woman sitting on a concrete stump, just rocking back and forth. In my spirit I immediately heard, "They are all around you; they are everywhere— you just can't see them."

My husband and I would soon get back together, but things weren't much easier. All our baggage and now even more trust issues compounded everything. There were many good days, too, but many storms were still to come. We tried counseling on and off, and we met with various pastors, but nothing seemed to help; in fact, it usually made things worse. We loved each other deeply, but we couldn't seem to fully forgive each other. I was very confused, and I knew that didn't come from God. I kept going, and I never stopped praying and seeking the Lord's will.

During this time in our lives, the older boys were in high school, and Noah was around six or seven. During one of our Sunday visits to Colorado Community Church, I saw a pamphlet from the Alternatives Pregnancy Center. I learned that they helped woman in unexpected pregnancy situations and provided Christian support and help to women who were forced to make decisions about unplanned pregnancies.

Wow, I thought, *this would be a great opportunity for me to give back and help other women through these difficult situations.* I signed up and enrolled in training sessions to become a volunteer. On the first day, the lovely woman interviewing me asked if I had ever had an abortion. I told her I had, and she asked me if I had ever received counseling for my abortion. I told her it had come up during some of my counseling sessions, and I also told her about being adopted and now having kids of my own. She told me I had a lot to offer, and I was excited to get started.

Now during this week, I had noticed, maybe overheard that one or two of the other women in the group had also been open about their past abortions with the group. I remember thinking that that was great and that they too were here to help other woman. Completely unbeknownst to me on what I believe was one of the last days of training, I learned the topic of discussion in my group for that day was going to be post-abortive syndrome (PAS). I had never heard of this before, but being a nurse, I knew of and had experienced firsthand PTSD.

As I read about the symptoms of post-abortive syndrome, I began experiencing physical symptoms— nervousness, anxiety, feeling like my entire body was overcome with emotion. As I looked at the list of symptoms one can experience after an abortion, I silently checked off each one in my heart, waiting for one or two that I had not experienced. My eyes welled up with tears and I just shut down. As far as I was concerned, I had been okay all these years—or had I?

I sat there stone-faced and tried not to let myself feel the pain. The minutes seemed to drag on and on, and I felt as though I was suffocating. I couldn't wait to run out of there and be alone in my car. Finally, it was time to be excused for the day, and I made it to my car as fast as I could.

On my way home, my eyes overflowed with tears, and I was completely overcome with emotion. I couldn't believe the level of pain I felt. All this time I thought I was okay. I had asked God for forgiveness multiple times, but this was different. I sobbed and screamed out of anger and hurt the entire way home.

I shared how I was feeling with my husband and one or two other people and then just allowed myself to grieve for the loss of this child, this baby, *my baby*, that I would never hold, never know. It was overwhelming, I had no idea the amount of pain I had shoved down so deep.

I experienced this extreme grief for several days. The Lord let me feel the full weight and gravity of what I had done—not to punish me, but to show me the truth. I was acutely aware that it didn't matter how early along the pregnancy was, the Lord showed me that at the moment of conception, the soul and spirit were already there—one week pregnant, six weeks pregnant, or eight months pregnant. When a woman is expecting a baby and loses that baby, we don't say, "Well, she was just a few weeks along"! The pain is the same no matter how far along she is; that was her baby, and she has a right to grieve that loss. But somehow when it's an abortion, it's "just a clump of cells"—a completely non-human being.

This lie is horrendous and has many consequences for us whether we choose to deal with them or not. The decision to end my baby's life with an abortion had affected me more negatively than anything else in my life by far. If sharing my story can keep one woman from not making the same decision that I did—by believing the lie that this abortion choice will somehow magically just "fix" this inconvenient problem—if one woman (or one man—men also suffer from PAS) can hear my story and listen to the other side, it will be worth it. If this is your situation, please know you're not alone; there are many men and woman who would do anything to help you.

Jesus is the great healer, and if you don't know him, that's okay, because he knows you. He is patient and the most loving, generous protector of your soul, and if you ask him to show you the truth and to help you heal, you can be sure he will.

After this experience, I realized that I was not ready to help other women just yet. I needed more years of healing, and the Lord would ever so slowly peel back the layers of wounds and scars that had built up and start healing them one by one. Lots of healing did take place, but more than ten years later, I would experience the most magical, amazing healing, but I still had a few big storms to get through.

CHAPTER 8

Detours

"You are the light of the world."

—Matthew 5:14

As I continued to work on strengthening my relationship with the Lord, a couple of huge boulders blocked my path and almost destroyed me, but first I want to share some amazing, life-changing moments the Lord allowed me to experience through my work as a hospice nurse. Throughout all my years as a hospice nurse, and some short stints in other areas such as jail nursing and pediatrics, the Lord has let me have the honor of sharing little pieces of him whenever possible. I will show you what I mean.

I never in a million years anticipated that the Lord would sometimes ask me to carry out certain things while "on the job." For instance, during my time as a jail nurse, I was overcome with the darkness and judgment directed at these men and woman. Instead of having an "innocent until proven guilty" attitude, most of the employees were very cynical and seemed to think they were better than the inmates.

I witnessed some heartbreaking things and had many opportunities to give messages to these men and women that perhaps their moms would have given them. I was able to warn them that prison was not the place they wanted to be. I would go into enough detail to let them know that this was a very dark and cold place, and I would tell them that I'd better not ever see them back here. They could see by the seriousness on my face and the tone in my voice that I was warning them out of love. They knew I truly cared, and they knew I was telling them the truth.

I would encourage them the best that I could in the sometimes just minutes of private time that I would have with them. In all the darkness they were going through (the Lord had let me experience this too, of course), I knew just what to say and just how to encourage them from all the cynical, evil that they were surrounded with. The look some of them would give me was pure shock, because in that darkness, the last thing they expected was a concerned, kind word coming from anybody. Yes, of course, there are some very bad people there. There were even times I could say I felt I was in a situation or around a person that could be considered evil and possibly dangerous. But the Lord protected me, and he also has other "undercover" workers of all capacities in prisons who do his work and spread his messages whenever needed. But to treat each person the same or with the attitude that my sins were so much better than theirs didn't feel right or appropriate.

I was asked many times why I was so nice and conversational with the inmates. For one, it helped me stay focused on my job at hand, which was medical assessments or medication administration, etc. But really, I knew that if I could make a difference in one person's life during some of their darkest days, then I was going to do that. If the Lord prompted me to encourage someone, offer a prayer, or even sometimes just give a smile, I was determined to follow that prompting, whatever the consequences.

"You are the light of the world. A city set on a mountain cannot be hidden. . . . Just so, your light must shine before others, that they may see your good deeds and glorify your heavenly Father." (Matthew 5:14,16)

I could never judge another person if I hadn't walked in their shoes. God's judgment will come upon us all, in his time, and in his way. Prayer and our Christian values are now surely under attack. We can see this all around us, but I would rather live a life trying to help others and praying than backing down when I know so many in this world are suffering.

Most of the times I felt led to pray were in nursing home or hospice settings. The first time this happened, I was working in a long-term care nursing home and had just received a report from the nurse going off shift. She explained that one man was currently on hospice care and scheduled to receive high doses of morphine every few hours to help manage his pain and shortness of breath. It was my first time ever taking care of a hospice patient, and I was a little apprehensive. As I walked in to give him his morphine a brief time later, he appeared to be close to dying. A brief time later, one of the CNAs let me know that the man indeed had passed away. I performed my assessment and then phoned the doctor. As I spoke with the doctor, I was overcome with emotion, and he asked, "Are you okay?"

I told him, "Well, I had just administered the morphine, and then he died." The doctor kindly assured me that this man was already dying, and that I was making sure he was comfortable and that that was a great thing. I was extremely thankful for the pep talk, and after this first time, similar things happened quite often.

Every time I had a dying patient that could no longer even speak, the Lord would tell me, "Pray with him or her."

I was shocked sometimes at the urgency and situations that I found myself in. I would kneel by the patient's head and pray with whatever words the Lord put in my heart. Sometimes there were specific things, but usually it was very straightforward, such as "If you don't already know the Lord, and if you agree in your heart . . ."

I always remember how vast God's love for souls is. No matter what kind of life we live, good or bad, or a mix of both, God is always there, especially when we die, giving us one last chance to turn toward him, if we haven't already. I felt privileged to be in the presence of a dying person, and I was always astounded at God's love for every soul, especially in their last days, hours, and minutes, and I would always pray for them myself.

The Lord revealed to me the spiritual battle each soul goes through at the time of death, and some of it left me completely in awe. As the years went on, some of the instances when the Lord would ask me to pray were a lot more urgent and very intense. I unfortunately have gone into homes in the middle of the night and have seen very dark things hung on walls—for instance, skulls covering entire walls. This house was very cold, and as I listened to confirm the absence of a heartbeat in a man who had already died, I felt as though an evil presence was standing behind me, causing the hairs on the back of my neck to stand up. Let's just say, I left those homes as soon as I possibly could.

Fortunately, there were many more positive experiences that I've encountered. The first of the two stories I will share is that of a man dying in the privacy of his own home. He did have some of what I call "dark décor," but he seemed nice enough and was really struggling to become comfortable. He had what is called "terminal agitation," a phenomenon in which someone becomes very restless in their last days or hours and almost no amount of medication can help.

My personal belief—and what the Lord has revealed to me over the years—is that there is a literal battle going on for every person's soul. And when the soul of the dying person hasn't already made up their mind, the battle seems to be much more intense. There are angels and demons fighting for every single soul until that soul's last dying breath. I needed to increase this particular man's pain and anxiety medications often, and I had been there for several hours at this point. Around two in the morning, he was up and down and seemed to be really suffering. He was sitting up on the edge of his hospital bed, and I could just feel life leaving him. I didn't think this man was the praying type, but I knew as uncomfortable as it might be, I needed to offer to pray.

In these situations, there was no time for a chaplain, priest, or social worker to show up, even if the person requested one. His partner was with us in the room, and I just blurted out, "Do you want me to pray with you?" Immediately I saw his partner smile as though I had said something ridiculous, and he said, "No, we are not religious!" But then, with all the strength he could muster, the patient said in the loudest, most assured voice said, "YES, please pray for me!" His partner's face registered pure and utter disbelief, and his jaw dropped open.

I sat down next to him on the bed, and holding his hand, I prayed. All I can remember is PEACE. The room was illuminated with a warm, glowing light and was filled the peace of God. It was one of the most beautiful moments I have ever been witness to. He died within minutes of my prayer, and I knew God had been with him! His partner cried and cried, but I saw a real peace come over him, and I knew that he had just witnessed the same thing I had. I stayed for a long time and tried to comfort and support him, but he was very quiet. His whole demeanor changed, and I knew he had experienced the overwhelming presence of God. I still pray for him to this day whenever I think of him.

The other situation I will share occurred in an inpatient hospice. I had only been working there two or three weeks and was still in training. Earlier on this particular shift, I made a mental note of one of the patients I noticed. She was in her mid-fifties or early sixties and was wearing a shirt with a joke on it that seemed sort of "out of place" for a hospice environment. Later, toward the end of my shift, this lady was having a terrible time. She hadn't moved or opened her eyes but was moaning out loud with pain and anxiety. Another nurse and I received new orders for high doses of medications to try and help her to become more comfortable. The nurse I was working with mentioned that the doses would be enough to "put down a horse."

Finally, the woman seemed to settle down a bit, and suddenly, I found myself standing alone at the head of her bed. The other nurse and two CNAs that had been in the room with me had quickly exited the room, and the door shut behind them. But we *never* closed a door; it always remained open unless a family member was there and closed it.

I turned back toward the patient, and immediately I heard the Lord say, "Pray for her." I was a little nervous—I was new at this job, and I knew anyone could open the door at any time. I silently explained to the Lord that this wasn't an ideal situation, but again I heard, "Pray for her" (in an even more serious tone). I hesitated again, until I heard for the third time, "Pray for her!" This was in the tone of your parent when you're about to get in trouble, and I was done arguing.

I began to pray, only this time something happened that had never happened before. It was as though the Holy Spirit was praying through me, and the words that I was saying were not coming from me at all. I was told to tell her that "Jesus is the truth, and what they are telling you is a lie!" Every time I spoke the name of Jesus, she had what appeared to be a mini seizure and began shaking. After I initially said this, she appeared to be shocked, like she was wondering how I knew what she was seeing. Of course, I didn't know, but God knew.

After I prayed this way several more times, she became calm and quiet. Suddenly, the room became extremely peaceful, and those same golden-like rays filled the room. As I turned toward the door, as I got ready to leave the room, still in shock of what had just happened, I could see the hazy outline of a very large angel standing in front of the door. I would guess the wingspan was around ten feet; I couldn't see the body, but I saw the wings. I just stood and stared at it until eventually it disappeared.

I made my way to the nurse's station, completely overwhelmed in so many ways. It was the end of our shift and time to give a report. I sat down with the other nurses, speechless and in shock. A few minutes later, several CNAs came to the nurse's station and said that the woman had passed away. One of the nurses said, "Oh, okay, thank you—we will be there in just a minute."

One of the CNAs insisted, "No, you don't understand—she was smiling, she was . . ." They were unable to put into words what they had witnessed. These CNAs had witnessed dozens of people pass away, but they could not put into words exactly what they witnessed and tried to explain it to us for several minutes. The parts that I could make out were that the patient was smiling when she died and seemed to be "seeing something."

As I drove home, still completely overcome with emotion, I just thanked the Lord. I was completely humbled and changed by this experience and many others throughout my nursing career. Please remember to pray for the dying and the ones who have gone before us, and never give up hope for anyone!

"The Lord is my shepherd, I shall not want. He makes me lie down in green pastures; He leads me beside quiet waters. He restores my soul; He guides me in the paths of righteousness for His name's sake. Even though I walk through the valley of the shadow of death, I fear no evil, for You are with me; Your rod and your staff, they comfort me. You prepare a table before me in the presence of my enemies; You have anointed my head with oil; My cup overflows. Surely goodness and lovingkindness will follow me all the days of my life, and I will dwell in the house of the Lord forever. (Psalm 23, NASB)

CHAPTER 9

The Great Fall

"Before I was afflicted I went astray, but now I hold to your promise."

—Psalm 119:6

I remember it like it was yesterday. Not long after I had been led to the Alternatives Pregnancy Center and received the beginning of much healing that would eventually come, I received a call from my dad. He had been diagnosed with lung cancer. I could hear in his voice how hesitant he was to tell me; he knew this would crush me. He said he had small cell lung cancer and would begin treatment soon. I had been attending online classes at Colorado Christian University and was getting close to obtaining my bachelor's degree in nursing. I immediately decided to quit school so I could be there for him as much as possible. Losing him was something I always knew was a real possibility, and it was now a reality.

The next two years I continued working as an on-call hospice nurse at night. I worked for a company that required me to work out of an office building in downtown Denver during my twelve-hour shifts. The Lord kept me safe during this time as I would travel all over town and work from the huge building all night alone. I felt unsafe a lot because of where the building was located, and the fact that I would be completely alone often entering and exiting the building at all hours of the night whenever patients or families needed me.

It was a lonely time for me. There were some family issues going on, and my best friend at the time, Dana, also had cancer. She was my night prayer sister during these months and was always there to pray with me and for my dad. Looking back, I prayed for her a lot, too, but she was so selfless and steadfast through her own cancer journey, always there for others before herself. She ended up dying before my dad did. She was only forty-two years old with two small boys. She was an absolute prayer warrior, and I will forever be grateful for her. I was told that when she died, her hands were raised in the air and she was smiling.

During this time of losing Dana and my dad continuing to battle cancer, the Lord was very protective of me. When I would leave for work, the Lord would give me little reports at the beginning of my shifts of what they would be like. He would sometimes say, "Tonight you will have no calls," which meant it would be a very long night alone in a huge, empty building, but less stressful overall. Other times he would say, "Tonight you will have two death visits," or he would let me know that a patient I had previously seen was now declining and would soon pass. This decreased my stress levels as it took away the not-knowing element of what my night would entail. I will never forget when I was working the night shift and sensed that Dad was having a rough time.

As soon as I had completed my shift and was back home, I called one of my uncles and asked him how my dad was doing. I will never forget the concern in his voice as he said, "Not good! Not good at all!" I was devastated and called a friend in tears. I wasn't allowed to be with Dad because a family member thought that because I was a hospice nurse, it would be too hard for me not to jump in and take over. Frankly, it would have been torture. As hard as that was, as I look back now, the Lord knew I wouldn't have been able to bear to see my dad suffer, and he protected me from that.

At the time we were going to a nondenominational church, but sometimes we visited Dana's Pentecostal church with her before she passed. During one of those services, I received two different messages for two different people. One was for a friend of my son; I heard the Lord say, "Tell Matt that I love him." I thought it was so sweet of him, and I said, "Okay, Lord." Then a second and third time the Lord repeated this message as though he was worried I might not take it seriously. I promised I would.

The second message was for my younger son's teacher, a single mom at the time; the Lord gave me a vision of her crying on her bed, and he told me to tell her she had a blessing coming. I knew in my spirit it was a husband, but I also knew I wasn't to tell her that. He specifically told me to tell her that "he sees you" and that she had a blessing coming. When I ran up to her to give her the message, as soon as I said, "The Lord told me to tell you that he *sees* you," she started trembling and crying. She seemed encouraged by the message, and within five or six months, she was married.

As for the friend of my son, I had to wait several days to tell him (and the Lord kept reminding me). Finally, I was in the car with my son, and I said, "Call Matt—the Lord gave me a message for him." Surprisingly, he didn't argue (he was in high school at the time) and called him immediately. When Matt answered, my son just told him that I had to talk to him. I was nervous—he was a teenager, and I was afraid how it might come across—but the Lord was insisting. I explained that this had never happened to me before, but that the Lord had asked me to give him a specific message. I went on and explained that three times the Lord told me to make sure and let him know how much he loved him.

A few seconds went by, and then Matt said, "You will never know how much I needed to hear that!" I was shocked . . . and so glad the Lord had persisted and hadn't let me forget. And through the years, the Lord has often put Matt in my heart, and I would pray for him.

The weeks and months that preceded my dad's passing were very emotional and worrisome times for me. I visited Dad every week and constantly prayed for him. The church we were attending at the time was very negative about the Catholic Church, especially when it came to praying to Mary or the concept of purgatory, and they even went as far as saying that Catholics weren't even Christians.

Years after my mom and dad had divorced, I learned that the Church had denied my dad's request for an annulment and then supposedly refused to baptize his new son after he had remarried (this was hearsay; I obviously didn't know any details). He had since turned his back on the Church, and since my stepmom didn't have any particular faith belief, my dad ended up away from God altogether. He might have had a personal prayer life, but if he did, he never spoke about it.

As it got closer to Dad's passing, I was terrified not knowing if he had made his peace with God. I gave

God many suggestions of what he could do to get my dad's attention and would beg and plead for God to just make sure he was all right (as if God really needed my suggestions). I refused to have a nonchalant attitude about something this serious. This was my dad and eternity we're talking about!

No other church that I know of besides the Catholic Church believes and teaches that purgatory is a place where the dying can go when they don't deserve hell but also do not die inside of the Lord's full graces. I've learned a lot about purgatory; it took me a very long time to believe in it. But to me, it ultimately is supporting evidence of our merciful, loving, and just God who desires us all to be with him for eternity. He wishes no one to reject him. In the *Catechism of the Council of Trent* on page 65 it states, "There is also the fire of purgatory, in which the souls of the pious are purified by a temporary punishment, that they may be admitted into their eternal country, into which nothing defiled entereth (Apoc. xxi. 27). And of the truth of this doctrine, which holy Councils declare to be confirmed by Scripture testimonies and Apostolical tradition (Trid. Concil. sess. 25)."

I knew Dad's heart and how much he loved all his children. I witnessed the tears that the pain of fractured relationships caused him over the years, and I saw how he never gave up on anyone and remained with immense love for all his children steadfastly, and no one could ever say or do anything to sway that love. I can honestly say that I never, ever heard him say a bad word about anyone! I'm not saying my dad was a saint, but he was a very good man.

The few times I tried to talk to him about God, he immediately would say, "I'm not religious, sweetie."

I'd reply, "I'm not either, Dad—I just want you to be at peace, that's all."

And with tears in my eyes, he would kindly assure me and say, "I am at peace, sweetie."

During our visits, I would always stop and get him something to eat if he was able, and then we would just sit and be together. It usually included watching either golf or football, and sometimes we would even get into politics, my dad always assuring me that no matter who was running or as bleak as it might look, I should always vote Republican, no matter what.

Occasionally he would refer to abortion, as there were ads on TV for some reason during a few of my visits (some even promoting late-term abortion), and say, "I don't believe in abortion; I think it's wrong." Then he would look at me with his concerned, kind eyes, and I would say, "I know, Dad, I don't either."

As the time got closer and closer to my dad's passing, he was signed up for hospice. I would often hear of his hospice nurse, Tom, but for some reason I never ended up running into him like I had suspected I would. I would ask Dad if he liked Tom, and he would say he did but wouldn't offer more details. One of the suggestions I had given God was that he could use Dad's hospice nurse to reach him. Another idea I had was having an angel appear to him—or possibly a preacher on the TV (as if God really needed my help!). I just knew in my heart it wasn't going to be me. I was his daughter, and he was my dad, and that's the way it was.

I had planted seeds and been able to offer up my prayers and ask others to pray alongside me, of course. I kept my faith as best I could as the days went on. And then, one day, I suddenly felt like I needed to confess some things to him and thank him for others. I knew his time was short. I told my dad about my abortion as the tears ran down my face, and he squeezed my hand trying to comfort me. I mostly thanked him for making me always feel so special and loved, and for adopting me. I also gave him a hard time and reminded him about the time he and my stepmom were having a garage sale and I found one of the tables covered with every single tie I had ever bought him! When I walked up to him that day with all those ties in hand, without missing a beat, he said, "Oh no! How did those get in there!" And we laughed and laughed.

A few days later, I had a strong feeling the end was getting closer, and I asked my boys if they wanted to miss school to say goodbye to "Big Grandpa." My two younger boys went with me, and it was a very sweet visit. Noah had colored a drawing of my dad playing football with him, and he wrote on it, "Dear Grandpa, I can't wait until I get to Heaven with you and we can play football together." My dad held it up, but it was upside down, so I straightened it out for him, and he just looked and looked at it. I eventually asked him if he wanted me to put it right next to him on the table, and with much seriousness in his voice he said, "Yes, right there." My middle son told him he loved him and got a hug too.

After a few minutes, the boys went outside, and I ended up alone with Dad. My heart was pounding, and the Lord softly hinted to my heart that this might be the last time I would be able to see him. I didn't know what to do. I didn't want to say goodbye, and then suddenly, I just knew. I took his hand, and he turned his head toward me, and I said, "Run to Jesus, Dad, run to Jesus!" There were no other words besides "I love you" that I needed him to hear. It was such a special moment. He looked up at me with his eyes shining and sparkling, and he gave me a funny smile as though I had done the unthinkable by bringing up Jesus. But this time, there was not one single ounce of his spirit that did not appear to be at absolute peace.

This would be the last time I spoke to my dad. He passed away on October 12, 2013, God rest his soul.

In the days and weeks to come, I was not doing well, and I was overcome with depression. I couldn't believe he was really gone. I decided to call my stepmom one day to see if I could have something of his—maybe a T-shirt, just anything I could keep. She said, "I have a huge bag of his clothes that I was about to give to Goodwill—do you want it?" I said yes and drove to her house to pick it up. When I opened the bag in the laundry room, I saw that many of the things were covered with dirt, so I decided to wash them. As I pulled out each item one by one, I checked the pants pockets for any money or paper that had possibly been left, as I always do with my family's laundry.

I was down to the very last piece of clothing: a single pair of jeans. Out loud, I started talking to my dad and said in a joking way, "Geez, Dad, you couldn't even leave me one single quarter!" And seconds later, as my hand was literally sliding into the pocket, my mouth dropped open. I felt one single coin, and I had a strong suspicion it was a quarter. It was. Even at arm's length, I could see, illuminating off the quarter, the words "In God We Trust." I started screaming with excitement, "Yes, Dad! In God we trust! In God we trust!" I was so thankful the Lord allowed that sign from my dad! That message brought me so much peace and joy in that moment.

Over the weeks that followed his death, however, I remained depressed and heartbroken. I felt like no one understood, not even my husband. I kept hearing the still, small voice of the Holy Spirit saying in my heart, "Call his hospice nurse." After about a month, I decided I would call the hospice organization and ask to speak with my dad's nurse so I could thank him for taking care of Dad. I will never forget when I received the call from Tom, Dad's hospice nurse. I thanked him for calling me back and explained I wasn't doing very well.

Immediately he told me, "Oh, I loved your dad so much!" He went on and on about how much he loved my dad, and that was so sweet. I then said, "I was praying so much and just really wanted him to be at peace. "Do you think my dad ever saw any angels?"

Tom said, "Oh, yes, your dad saw lots of angels!" Tom then shared with me that he had been a medic in the army and that he was a devout Catholic. When I heard the Catholic part, I felt a little worried and wondered if

Catholic prayers were effective—but he did call himself a "prayer warrior." Yes, the bad things and misinformation I was told about Catholics had really taken a toll on me, and my memories being in the church as a young girl and every other weekend were just fading memories. By this time, I had been away from the Catholic faith for many decades.

Tom then said, "Oh, your dad loved to pray!"

I literally nearly dropped the phone. "Are you serious!? My dad prayed with you?"

"Oh, yes, he would put his hands together on his chest, and when I would finish, he would say, "Thank you so much; that was very nice."

I could hardly believe my ears. We went on to enjoy the loveliest conversation. Tom and I kept in touch for years after that, and I'm so thankful that he relayed that information to me; it gave me so much hope and comfort.

After that, I just tried to go on the best I could, and I cried a lot. My husband would try to help and say, "He's in a better place" or "He's happy now, and he wants you to be happy" and I would just get more upset and tell him I didn't want to talk about it. Unfortunately, looking back now, I should have sought grief counseling. I did go to one session offered by the hospice, but it was not an ongoing program.

Looking back now, with some perspective, it's easy to see that I had complicated and compounded grief with other things I had been going through, even besides my marriage. I now know that this kind of despair is a sin, because it goes beyond the normal sorrow or sadness we all experience. But when we despair, we have started giving up what hope we have left, and that leads us away from God.

I pushed through but felt myself continue to break a little more each day. During one of the only times I heard from the Lord in the midst of all this, he told me to read Psalm 119 every day. I started to read it, but I just kept thinking it seemed to take me a long time to get through it. One day I was talking to a pastor, and I mentioned that I was trying to read Psalm 119 every day. He said, "Really? That's the longest psalm in the Bible, with 176 verses." Here is an example of a beautiful excerpt from this psalm and how God was trying to speak to me:

"Let my cry come before you, Lord; in keeping with your word, give me understanding. Let my prayer come before you; rescue me according to your promise. May my lips pour forth your praise, because you teach me your statutes. May my tongue sing of your promise, for all your commandments are righteous. Keep your hand ready to help me, for I have chosen your precepts. I long for your salvation, Lord; your law is my delight. Let my soul live to praise you; may your judgements give me help. I have wandered like a lost sheep; seek out your servant, for I do not forget your commandments." (Psalm 119:169-176)

Looking back now, I guess I can say that my heart had maybe hardened a bit. My spirit was sinking deeper and deeper; I was barely hanging on. Eventually I decided to give myself a break from hospice and signed on to work for a pediatric home care agency. This was a little less stressful, although I didn't like it as much. But eventually I was put with a little angel baby, and her sweet smiles and angelic looks were a balm to my aching soul.

In the weeks to come, as I was feeling so weak and low, unbeknownst to me, I was walking right into a trap set by the enemy. As much as I can't stand to give him credit, I must admit, he had a well-thought-out and well-executed plan. He was the perfect enemy of my soul; he had thought everything through and took care of every detail. He knew the time to strike was when I was at my lowest point and in deep despair. He knew the exact weapons to use against me, and he was counting on me to stay where I was spiritually: not in the Word daily, no regular prayer time, and mourning the loss of both my best friend/encourager and my dad.

One night while I was working, my new boss called and began asking me questions about my assignment. To my surprise, he was very talkative and started telling jokes and making me laugh. I couldn't remember the last time I had laughed. It was such a feeling of being liberated from the constant wretched pain I'd been feeling. Of course, it all started out innocent—the evil one had to make it innocent, or I never would have taken the bait.

Over the next couple of weeks, the calls from my boss became more frequent, and we seemed to have more conversations than are appropriate between a boss and his employee. At first, I kept my boundaries. I rationalized his advances by talking about God and bring up Christian topics. But it didn't matter; no matter how many times I turned down his advances, he was relentless and didn't stop. The thing that got me was that it was a welcome distraction for me, a reprieve from the constant pain I felt. I did see the obvious red flags, but because of my pride, I deceived myself, and my fatal mistake was that I thought I was in control.

The Lord tried hard to intervene, giving me many warnings and signs to stop talking to this person. Unfortunately, I continued to dig my feet in and continued to tell myself that I was in control. I knew that if I stopped, all the pain would come rushing back, and I didn't think I could handle that. It was too painful, and I didn't feel strong enough.

During this time, the enemy knew I had serious doubts about my marriage lasting and had contemplated divorce many times. He was still relentless with the constant spiritual warfare in my marriage, and I was still extremely disappointed and hurt by my husband about many things in the past that I couldn't seem to let go of. My husband had crossed many lines and this had obviously done much damage to our relationship. But whether I had been considering divorce or not, it still didn't justify the situation with my boss.

Then, one day I wasn't up to going in for my shift, and I was dreading calling my boss. When I called him to tell him to cancel my shift, before he could even get mad, I told him I would meet him for a drink. Of course, he was happy with that. I had made the final move that would end in much destruction to my marriage and hurt many of my relationships.

Of course, the drinks were the final weapon of choice for the enemy. In a short amount of time, I had, against my better judgment, allowed myself to be in a position where something very bad could happen, and it did. It was my choice to drive and meet my boss alone for a drink. The truth is that, as much as I would love to make excuses for my decision, I can't, and it was an instantaneous regret.

After we parted for the evening, I was very intoxicated and still had to drive home. This was the second time that I would drive while intoxicated to this point. But even through this, the Lord got me safely home. I will never forget how the steering wheel would do a hard jerk to wake me up and swerve us back into the lane (yes, us—myself and my guardian angel). Once again, why would God save me? Especially when I was living in sin, living outside of his will, and trying to numb my pain in the worst of all possible ways.

The next morning I woke up hungover, ashamed, and humiliated and lower than I ever had been before. I heard the whispers of the devil telling me, "Now I've got you! Now you will not be able to do anything for God!" He knew the shame I was carrying would absolutely crush me, and it did, it really did.

I fell into sin doing something I had judged others harshly for. Don't ever think of yourself as so strong or righteous that you don't have to worry about committing certain sins that you are certain you could never commit. Because God forbid you ever find yourself there like I did. I felt that weight of that sin every day, and the aftermath was very ugly and compounded my grief and pain even more. I hurt many people I never wanted to hurt, ever. To those of you who were hurt by any of the choices I have made, if I haven't already told you, I am deeply sorry. You know who you are, and I pray you can forgive me. I love you so very much.

"Do not merely listen to the word, and so deceive yourselves. Do what it says. Anyone who listens to the word but does not do what it says is like a man who looks at his face in the mirror and, after looking at himself, goes away and immediately forgets what he looks like. But the man who looks intently into the perfect law that gives freedom, and continues to do this, not forgetting what he has heard, but doing it, he will be blessed in what he does." (James 1:22)

"Speak and act as those who are going to be judged by the law that gives freedom, because judgement without mercy will be shown to anyone who has not been merciful. Mercy triumphs over judgment!" (James 2:12)

Within weeks of this, I was at home one night and had opened a bottle of wine. I didn't intend to go anywhere;

I just planned to stay at home alone. As I opened the bottle, I heard the Lord say, "No more."

I had the audacity to question the Lord's concern and exclaimed that I was not going to be leaving the house. He continued, "Everything bad that has ever happened to you has been when you were drinking alcohol."

Immediately all the memories came rushing into my mind, especially the times my life was spared, and I put the bottle down and said, "Yes, Lord, I'm so sorry!" Since that evening, I would be lying if I said I never touched alcohol again, but in the eight years or so since, I can only think of maybe three times. And I can happily say it's been years now. I don't really struggle anymore with craving it, but like everyone else who has been an alcoholic, I guess what they say is that you always are one, and I thank the Lord that he has helped me overcome this.

According to Jessie Romero, who has significant training in spiritual warfare and also wrote the book *The Devil in the City of Angels*, there are "three doorways modern man is opening himself up to the diabolical" and one of the ways is through alcohol and drugs. To summarize, he says that "demons love this because now your intellect and mind are compromised, your intellect and will are compromised and seized by the devil." And then he explains how you follow your emotions, which most of the time are disordered.[4]

The other thing the Lord showed me during the aftermath of my fateful decision and all the pain and heartache is that it added to the old wounds that my husband and I had never fully healed from. One day, when it was all very recent, I was torturing myself trying to figure out what to do with the state that my marriage was in. I was exhausted from how hard the marriage had been, and I just couldn't imagine that my husband or I would or should continue fighting to hold on to our marriage.

One day, though, the Lord gave me a profound revelation. I was walking down the stairs in our townhouse, considering divorce again. When I was halfway down the stairs, I suddenly heard the Lord say (very matter-of-factly), "You can get divorced, but this is how you will feel." Immediately I was overcome with intense emotions of sadness, depression, regret, and loneliness.

And then the Lord said, "And this is how Noah will feel," and he let me feel my son's completely broken heart. It was unimaginable; I couldn't stand to feel my son suffering! The idea was utterly unbearable! I knew right then that there was absolutely no way I could put my son

---

4 Jesse Romero's words are paraphrased from a YouTube video the author watched that featured him.

through that, and I also realized that I would suffer greater regret and depression than ever before. I was stunned that the Lord allowed me to have this huge grace.

The other defining moment during this time was an experience the Lord gave me one night when I was working a night shift caring for a sweet baby girl. It was very close to the time I had fallen into sin, and I was ruminating on everything that had transpired. Suddenly, I was overcome with a sense of overwhelming anxiety, and I began to fear the possibility of God maybe not forgiving me.

And then I heard in my spirit, "This is what it would feel like if you were completely separated from me." Within seconds I was in complete and utter darkness; there was absolutely no light in the level of hell I was in. I couldn't see anything, even if it was directly in front of my face. I was completely and utterly aware of where I was and why I was there, and there was a constant stream of the same agonizing thoughts that tormented my mind nonstop. I was overcome with depression, anxiety, and extreme regret because I *knew* I was there forever—for eternity. Deep, deep sadness. Negative emotions flooding my consciousness, like a record playing over and over in my head. And I felt what being separated 100 percent from God feels like. Without God, there is no love, no forgiveness, no safety, no peace—even boredom would be a reprieve. It's just complete and utter despair and a darkness that never ends.

It was utterly terrifying, and I wouldn't wish it on my worst enemy. It's unimaginable to me that a soul who turns away from God or who chooses mortal sin and doesn't repent could end up eternally separated from God. I cannot put into words how utterly horrific this is. They say that God doesn't send anyone to hell; we choose it for ourselves ultimately with our actions and choices. I have a fear, though, that many people don't believe that hell exists, and I am here to tell you that it does—and I pray you don't go there.

I have a journal entry dated September 19, 2021, that reads:

What I would encourage others who might be questioning if something in their life was okay with God is first, obviously look to Holy Scripture, and then most of all, especially when society now tells us that everything is permissible, go directly to the source. God will reveal his thoughts and desires for your life. When asked with humility and a sincere yearning for truth and the desire to be in God's good graces, he will never leave you questioning or wondering. He will always answer.

We can be sure HE knows what's best for us and loves us more than we can understand. We have to keep the perspective that we are here on this earth for a brief moment in time, and where we will spend eternity is what really needs to weigh heavy upon our hearts. I have learned that there are lots of holy people foregoing all sorts of short-term happiness deals in the here and now for eternity and all its beauty and splendor. Eternity is their promise and anchor for the time being. We will learn that serving and giving and forgiving are some of the most treasured things we can do and receive.

In Thomas Aquinas' *Summa Theologica*,[5] he taught that hell is reserved for the wicked and the unbaptized immediately after death, but that those who die only in original sin will not suffer in hell. Aquinas also taught that, on Judgment Day, the punishment of hell will consist of fire and of "whatever is ignoble and sordid," since "all the elements conduce to the torture of the damned," who "placed their end in material things." Aquinas further taught that the worm of the damned is a guilty conscience, that the damned will suffer over

---

5 These quotes from *Summa Theologica* can be found on https://en.m.wikipedia.org/wiki/Hell_in_Catholicism.

the fact of having separated themselves from God, that the damned will physically weep on Judgment Day, that hell is so full of darkness that the damned can only see things that will torment them, that the "disposition of hell" is "utmost unhappiness," that the fire of hell is non-physical (before Judgment Day) and physical (at Judgment Day), that the physical fire of hell will not be made of matter, and that whether or not hell is under the earth is unknown. Aquinas taught that the suffering of punishment is according to one's sins, so that some will suffer more, in deeper and darker pits of hell, than others."

To say that this vison was the most terrifying experience of my life would be a huge understatement. This is my why. This is why I will never stop striving for Heaven and talking about God and Jesus for the rest of my days. I will never again take for granted the good times when I am in God's good graces because I know how hard the devil tries to drag us to hell. I know until Jesus comes back, none of us are free from the devil's schemes.

Please never say that you are too smart or too close to God to fall into one of his traps like I did. Studying the Holy Word of God, being in constant prayer, and regularly receiving the Sacraments and sacramentals given to us by the Catholic Church are the most powerful weapons against Satan. Also, I would come to soon know the power of the Most Holy Blessed Mother and the many prayers we have been given (especially when we can't find our own words).

Now, since many years have gone by, I can see clearly why the Lord bestowed this great grace and mercy on me. He knew the best thing for all of us was for Hans and me to stay together, but he also knew the enemy wasn't going to make it an easy road for us.

Little did I know I was about to embark on quite the journey of redemptive suffering, healing, and growing in my faith and receiving amazing graces from God. Many days I was just fighting to hang on, literally feeling like I couldn't stand the pain another minute and wanting to die, and other days I was filled with astounding graces and God's great mercy and love, all underneath the shelter of the Lord's protection.

On Christmas Day 2022, the Lord helped me to understand that all the different times I have fallen into sin were severe attacks from the enemy, but now, after so much healing, it's much easier for me to navigate life and see things more clearly. Did I know right from wrong? Absolutely! Do I take full responsibility for my part in my transgressions? Of course. But the Lord explained that when you are suffering with mental illness, depression, anxiety, and even more extreme, compounded traumas, you are often merely given a surface remedy, but many doctors or counselors never get to the root of the problems or encourage the much-needed healings. They medicate or charge you to tell them the hard things you've gone through. Sometimes medications are necessary, and they can even save lives, so I would never discourage taking them. But I would encourage to continue to seek the Lord, who is our ultimate healer.

The Lord explained it to me this way. He showed me a picture of a huge storm in my mind's eye. He placed me standing right in the middle of the storm. He said, "When you were inside the storm, it was impossible for you to interpret anything correctly. The wind and storms surrounded you, and you had no way to know what was what or which way to go." Then he added, "Now that you're standing outside of the storm, you have a clarity that you had never had before." As I've been on my journey and grown closer to him, the Lord has allowed me to heal from many things and allowed me to see things much clearer. I still suffer from depression and anxiety at times and am continuing to draw near to the Lord and seek his guidance in these sensitive and very important matters.

Without God, many cannot endure the sufferings of life alone. I realized that with God's help and comfort and the peace we can't get from anyone or anywhere else, I could make it through crippling depression, anxiety, and the scariest of spiritual warfare attacks. Without God, our absolute lifeline, when faced with horrendous pain, our souls and spirits cannot hang on and sustain us against the devil, who is relentless in wanting to harm us in any way he can—hence the rising number of suicides and mental illness.

The devil's biggest lie (after trying to convince us that he doesn't even exist) is telling us that something is wrong with us when we are suffering and that no one else is suffering the way we are. He wants us to feel isolated in our suffering and feel ashamed and embarrassed about it. He wants us to keep it to ourselves because he knows that any human soul can only take so much until they reach the breaking point. But our loving Heavenly Father will never leave us alone. He is always there, just waiting for us to ask for his assistance, his help, his protection.

Trust him! God is the most perfect, loving, concerned Father, and he cares for you more than you will ever know. When a child is lost, our Heavenly Father will never rest, never stop searching, never stop pursuing until his child is found and safe.

Please pray daily for all the suffering souls who are on the verge of suicide. Prayer is free— there is no limit, and it's the most powerful thing you can do. There are many, many people all over the world suffering great horrendous atrocities; they are often forgotten and need our prayers.

> "Not only so, but we also glory in our sufferings, because we know that suffering produces perseverance, perseverance, character, and character, hope. And hope does not put us to shame, because God's love has been poured out into our hearts through the Holy Spirit, who has been given to us." (Romans 5:3-5, NIV)

The Lord was about to lead my husband and me down a very specific path that I was not prepared for, all while leading me through my own redemptive suffering and journey to healing. I wish I could say it was easy to trust him in the process, but it wasn't. Many days I was sure we were off course or thought I might have misinterpreted something. It felt like such a lonely, dark world at times, but God knew exactly what it would take to bring me to a vulnerable place where I had no choice but to fully surrender and rely on him literally every minute of every day. And then it all began.

May your face always shine upon me . . .

I hid my face from you, my very source of life
I hid my face from you, throughout the day and night
I know when you are near, and when we are close
I feel the dark weight of the adversary glooming all
around
It never fails, like a moth stuck to honey, if you are near,
there he lurks, waiting
Just waiting for my slip, my trip, then he comes in with
a vengeance, ever so cunning,
The purest form of evil
Day after day the weight I bear, when will I learn to
give it all to you?
My protector, my Savior, I've let you down again....
How I don't deserve your love or forgiveness....
I hide my face from you, and I feel the
weight lifted...
I can take a deep breath and drink in the stability of the
lovely deceiving world...
For a while I feel better until, until I can't shut out your
voice longing for me.
I can't erase the image of the love you have for me
imprinted on my heart...

Father, please forgive me, please don't leave me for I am
so lowly and weak.
To think I can survive away from you, your protection,
for an hour, one minute.
Please don't hide your face from me, please come back
to thee that loveth and adores you.
Like a father disciplining his child, with loving hands
and a loving heart.
Please teach me to fully understand the ramifications of
hiding my face from your love.
Please don't let me be fooled or brought so weary.
Please leave no other option than you and me forever
reaching for each other's faces...
How I long to see your face, please don't turn away.
Please come back and stay forever in my heart, even if
the weight crushes me.
You know what's best, please discipline me father.
Please keep me safe, your daughter.

CHAPTER 10

Into the Wilderness

"Have mercy on me, God, in accord with your merciful love; in your abundant compassion blot out my transgressions. Thoroughly wash away my guilt; and from my sin cleanse me. For I know my transgressions; my sin is always before me. Against you, you alone have I sinned; I have done what is evil in your eyes so that you are just in your word, and without reproach in your judgement. Behold, I was born in guilt, in sin my mother conceived me. Behold, you desire true sincerity; and secretly you teach me wisdom. Cleanse me with hyssop, that I may be pure; wash me, and I will be whiter than snow. You will let me hear gladness and joy; the bones you have crushed will rejoice. Turn away your face from my sins; blot out all my iniquities. A clean heart create for me, God; renew within me a steadfast spirit. Do not drive me from before your face, nor take from me your holy spirit."

—Psalm 51:3-13

One night, out of the blue, my husband mentioned to me that he had been researching the Catholic Church for the past six months. He said it first started out of curiosity when the nondenominational church we had been attending had spoken badly about Catholics and it made him think of his parents and family in Chile, who were Catholic.

We had both been baptized Catholic as infants, and we had both attended Mass as children, but it didn't really go beyond that much. My husband knew I was very anti-Catholic after being in the Church of Christ and other denominations where I was taught that it was wrong to pray to Mary. I also had objections with confession and insisted that we could go straight to Jesus—we didn't need any priest to confess our sins to.

Apparently, he started having dreams and visions of bishops and popes and beautiful gardens, and after he felt the Holy Spirit's promptings and felt comfortable he wouldn't be leading us astray, he was ready to share his thoughts with me. He said he hadn't found anything wrong with the theology and was feeling led to return to the Catholic Church.

He told me about a conversation he had with a pastor from our nondenominational church about the Eucharist (which Catholics believe to be the true presence of Jesus). The pastor asked, "If it truly is Jesus, why don't they do it every day?"

And my husband said, "They do!"

"Amen, amen, I say to you, whoever believes has eternal life. I am the bread of life. Your ancestors ate the manna in the desert, but they died; this is the bread that comes down from heaven so that one may eat it and not die. I am the living bread that came down from heaven; whoever eats this bread will live forever; and the bread that I will give is my flesh for the life of the world." The Jews quarreled among themselves, saying, "How can this man give us [his] flesh to eat?" Jesus said to them, "Amen, amen, I say to you, unless you eat the flesh of the Son of Man and drink his blood, you do not have life within you. Whoever eats my flesh and drinks my blood has eternal life, and I will raise him on the last day. For my flesh is true food, and my blood is true drink. Whoever eats my flesh and drinks my blood remains in me and I in him." (John 6:47-56)

Soon enough, my husband would divulge all his research during the time he had spent reflecting and considering on the Catholic Church. I will never forget my stark reaction to him the first time he broached the subject with me. We had just gone through some of the biggest storms and were still living in the aftermath of all the garbage that it stirred up. I was standing in the kitchen, and he told me he had attended Mass a few times.

I said, "What? Are you kidding me?" I thought, *Now things really couldn't get any worse!*

He kept his composure and calmly said, "Kelli, all the people you have been closest to in your life have been Catholic." As much as I wanted to come up with a good comeback, as soon as he said that, my grandma, papa, dad, and mom just started encircling my heart. It was like an arrow straight to my heart. It was true—how could I have never thought of this before?

I said begrudgingly, "I will go to a Mass with you." He told me that I needed to go to confession before I received Communion. I was so stubborn and reminded him that I had been raised Catholic and had made my first Communion and Confirmation, so if I wanted to receive Communion I surely could.

He then said, "Kelli, you do know that Catholics believe that Jesus is truly present in the Eucharist, right?"

"What are you talking about?" I snapped. "You mean like a symbol, right?"

"No, not as a symbol—Catholics believe that Jesus is truly present in the Eucharist—his body and blood, soul and divinity."

I said, "Oh my gosh, that's crazy! Of course, it's symbolic!"

He then proceeded to show me all the Eucharistic miracles that have been researched and studied all over the world. I had never even heard of such a thing! These were blind, unbiased studies done by varying scientists and scholars. I was shocked and immediately thought, *If this is true, why isn't it on the news? Why aren't people talking about it all over the world? Why doesn't everyone know about this?*

Saint John Paul II says this about the Eucharist:

United with the angels and saints of the heavenly Church, let us adore the *Most Holy Sacrament of the Eucharist*. Prostrate, we adore this great mystery that contains God's new and definitive covenant with humankind in Christ.[6]

This was a huge deal! How did I grow up Catholic and not know about this? I was confused and somewhat eager to go to Mass, but I also was stubborn and not going to confession. I had confessed all my sins to God himself;

---

6 St. Pope John Paul II, *We Adore God Present Among Us*, Papal Document, accessed on EWTN.com, https://www.ewtn.com/catholicism/library/we-adore-god-present-among-us-8183.

I had a relationship with him and didn't feel the need to go through a priest.

So we went to Mass, and I received Communion for the first time in probably twenty-four years! When we got home, I felt a bit grouchy, and my husband said, "It's probably because you received Communion without going to confession." I didn't understand. Wouldn't Jesus just be glad I was there? I really didn't understand what telling a priest all my personal sins would to do.

I was in good company, though. As an article titled "The Grave Danger of Receiving the Eucharist Unworthily"[7] states:

> A Pew study from 2019 reflected the sad reality that only 31 percent of Catholics believe the bread and wine at Mass become the actual body and blood of Jesus. In other words, 69 percent of Catholics do not believe in the Real Presence, which is the *source and summit of the Christian life* (CCC, 1324). Understanding the Eucharist and the judgement one can bring upon themselves when receiving it

7 Amelia Monroe Carlson, "The Grave Danger of Receiving the Eucharist Unworthily," January 27, 2020, Catholic365, https://www.catholic365. com/article/11025/the-grave-danger-of-receiving-the-eucharist-unworthily. html#:~:text=When%20you%20receive%20the%20Eucharist,and%20 danger%20upon%20the%20unbeliever.

unworthily is essential because it's the only sacrament that brings a judgement if it is received unworthily.

The article goes on to say "To receive any sacrament of the church in mortal sin is to commit a sacrilege, which, as the *Baltimore Catechism* points out, is 'a great sin, because it is an abuse of a sacred thing.'" I obviously had no idea at the time, (even though my husband tried to explain this to me). The Lord knew, though, that we both separately and together needed the sacraments to nourish, protect, heal, and sanctify us.

After reading about the Eucharistic miracles, I just knew it had to be true; there was no way our Heavenly Father would ever let us be deceived about something this important. Our Heavenly Father loves us so much that he didn't leave us to fight all these spiritual battles alone. This newfound truth of the Eucharist was absolutely life-changing for me, and I believe the Lord bestowed a blessing on me for my belief and reverence for the Most Holy Eucharist after that.

Around this time, my husband and I both took new jobs and moved north of Denver to Broomfield. One night Hans was working, and Noah and I went to an evening Mass at the Immaculate Heart of Mary Catholic Church in Broomfield. It was such a beautiful Mass, with dim lighting and candles. For some reason, that evening

I was questioning whether it was okay for me to receive Communion. In the quiet and privacy of my mind, I told Jesus before receiving Communion, "Lord, I feel like I need to receive you—I need your strength and protection and your nourishment—but if there's any reason that you are not okay with it, then please give me a sign and I will only receive the blessing." I made it up to the front of the line, and my heart and spirit were overcome with love from Jesus. I turned to the Eucharistic minister who was helping distribute Holy Communion, and when I looked up at her face, it was glowing, and there was a bright light radiating from her eyes. I believed it to be the Holy Spirit, and I was overcome with emotion and love for my Lord.

I had been struggling with insomnia, and severe prolonged anxiety that would not give me any reprieve. Each day when I woke up, I was used to feeling this acute, prolonged anxiety as soon as my eyes opened. It was torturous! But after going to sleep that night, when I opened my eyes and sat up in bed the next morning, I immediately was aware that the anxiety was gone. I was overwhelmed by the peacefulness I felt instead. As my feet touched the floor, my body was filled with more of this great peace. With each step, there was an orange-yellowish soft glowing light in the room, and the peacefulness was so strong and overwhelming that it felt like I was on drugs (or what I assume some drugs might feel like), but I had absolutely no medication of any kind in my system.

I was supposed to be getting ready for work, but the peace was so overwhelming that I couldn't. I wasn't sure exactly what was happening to me; I almost felt as if I was floating. I called my husband who was driving home from a night shift and explained to him what I was experiencing. He immediately said, "Oh wow, it sounds like you're having a mystical experience or something!"

I had no idea what that was. When we got off the phone, I said out loud, "Lord, if you want me to get ready for work, you're going to have to dial this down a little bit."

Immediately upon me stating this out loud, the peace and love started to slowly dissipate and became just a soft glow. I was then able to focus on preparing for work. It was the most overwhelming peace, and after that, I never questioned that the Holy Eucharist was Jesus himself. I knew this experience of great peace had something to do with the great reverence and love I offered to the Lord before receiving Holy Communion, and I am forever thankful to him. He is so good, and all deserving of our love.

During this time, Noah and Hans were in classes to receive their First Communion and Confirmation. Hans and I were learning new things about the Catholic faith every day, even though we both felt the constant spiritual warfare. During this time there was very little reprieve from the suffering I felt. I didn't know how or if I was going to make it through it some days, but the Lord knew, and he protected and sustained me during this extremely hard time.

My first job after moving to Broomfield was case management for hospice. I loved my patients so much, but the amount of stress was just too much. When my hair started falling out week by week, my husband suggested that I apply for something less stressful. I ended up switching jobs and went on to work for a couple years with adults who had been injured or sustained cancers or other illnesses working in the mines or other various jobs near Louisville, Colorado. I ended up working for two different families whose homes became like second homes to me during this stressful time. When you work twelve hour shifts in someone's home, they become like family to you. These were both such loving and kind families, and I felt safe being with them and sometimes felt they did more for me than I was doing for them.

Without the unwavering love from my boys and my husband and my Heavenly Father directing my steps ever so carefully, I can't say for sure I would have made it through this time. I was plagued with nightmares and visions of myself walking across train tracks (we lived next to train tracks at the time). The pain from all my wounds were still festering, and my marriage wasn't magically fixed overnight.

At times the pain was so bad that I wanted to die, but I knew that wasn't an option. I didn't want to be away from my children, but the pain that the Lord would let me experience felt crushing and too much to bear at times. Still to this day I occasionally experience this kind of pain. Now looking back, I can see how the Lord was chipping away at the layers of pain each day. He has revealed so much to me since this time regarding suffering, so it makes it more bearable and easier for me to understand.

Journal Entry, November 12, 2021

In your weakness you are strong.

You are strong because of your weakness, not despite it. It's not as the world teaches or thinks. In your weakest most vulnerable moments, I am there, I am infusing myself to you and strengthening you from the inside out and bringing you into what you were made for, protecting you and giving you the exact right amount of strength that you need for this day. Not too much and not too little. In your times of "weakness and vulnerability," think of it differently. You are not weak; the Holy Spirit can do his work that I need him to do only in these moments. The more you can remain in this state with great humility, the better off you will be. Remain in me, and I remain in you. I love you. You are special too. You are my daughter, so lift up your eyes to me and keep them on me. No tear goes uncounted. You're on the right path; keep going and push through the gate. I know you feel like you cannot breathe, but you cannot see how close you are! My daughter, you are almost there. I am so proud of you, and I love you too. Again, remain in me always.

Every day I would trust him just a little more, learn something new about the faith, and grow in my prayer life. I was so fragile that I decided to go to Mass most days during the week as well as on the weekend. During Mass, I knew I was being healed and strengthened by the Eucharist and by being in the Lord's presence. I would often go to Mass after working a twelve-hour night shift, and I would cry through most of it. I thought the suffering and sadness were never going to end, but somehow, I knew that if I kept showing up, I would be protected and receive the strength and healing to keep going.

Daily Mass is amazing because it's attended by people who really desire to be with Jesus as much as possible, and the reverence and peace you feel is multiplied. I felt safety in seeing the familiar faces each day; we all had our seats, and it was a little bit of heaven on earth. In the Mass, there is a veil, a protective covering. The cold hard world outside was kept at bay while I rested in the arms of our savior.

On my days off and on the weekends when Hans was working, Noah and I got to spend so many special days together. One day, while we were watching television, we stumbled across a show on EWTN called *The Journey Home*. This show was instrumental in my reversion back to Catholicism.

This was when the sex abuse scandals in the Church were in the news, and I was so sad and angry about this. How could these evil things happen in the *Church*? My husband was so amazing and patient during these times; he would remind me that the Catholic Church, like all other churches, was not immune to evil. We are still in the world, and until Jesus comes back, the devil will try to cause brokenness—*especially* in the Catholic Church, being that it is the home of Jesus Our Lord, in the Most Holy Sacrament. Satan worshipers will attend Masses just to try and steal the consecrated host (at times successfully). I've heard ex-Satan worshipers (like Zackary King, for instance) tell of the great sacrilege they committed against the Most Holy Eucharist when they performed their black masses. Satan worshipers know that Jesus is truly present, and that's why they attempt to desecrate the Most Holy Eucharist whenever they can.

I watched episode after episode of *The Journey Home*, amazed at how the Lord had led so many people either back into the Catholic Church or into it for the first time. So many of them admitted they didn't even think Catholics were Christians. It was so comforting to hear stories from every race and religion, including many amazing testimonies from faithful Muslims and Jews. Every time the enemy would try and plant a doubt in my mind about the Church, all it took was watching another episode, and the peace would immediately come back.

Catholic radio also was instrumental during this time. I felt so moved while listening to these testimonies and learning about the sacraments. I remember asking the Lord, "Lord, which is it? Which is more important, a personal relationship with you or the sacraments?" And I heard, as clear as day, "Both." Of course, it was both! He knew the spiritual battle we would be in.

Shortly after moving, we turned in the paperwork to get my first marriage annulled so we could then get our marriage blessed in the Catholic Church and receive the Sacrament of Holy Matrimony. "When the Catholic Church teaches that marriage between two baptized persons is a sacrament, it is saying that the couple's relationship expresses in a unique way the unbreakable bond of love between Christ and his people."[8]

During this year, my husband and I were instructed to live as "brother and sister" until we had our marriage convalidated, or blessed, in the Church. This was a time for each of us to focus on God separately and together and to embrace marriage with a fresh start in a new sacramental bond.

One day my husband came home with several rosaries in his pocket. In the beginning, I had a very hard time with Mary. I didn't understand the obsession many Catholics had with the Blessed Mother; it often seemed to me as being a little off-putting to Jesus. I had no desire to pray the rosary—how could I? Jesus had all my love and attention, and there was no one else who deserved any love or affection, I thought. But when Hans brought home the rosaries, I decided to go into my big walk-in closet and talk to the Lord. For three days I prayed and begged the Lord to show me the truth about Mary and what he thought about praying the rosary. I explained to him that I didn't want to do anything that he was not okay with, or anything disrespectful. I absolutely

8 https://linusparish.com/ministries/7-sacraments/sacrament-holy-matrimony.

would not be comfortable I explained to him, unless he personally gave me a sign—I had to be sure it was okay with him!

That same week, Hans, Noah, and I had driven up to the Immaculate Heart of Mary, the parish where Hans and Noah were in their classes and the main parish where we attended Mass. As we walked in, to the right there were many beautiful candles lit and a kneeler to pray. I decided to kneel down and say a prayer for my boys like I always did. Out of the corner of my eye, I saw that a statue of Mary was directly in front of me. I hesitated, but then I just reminded myself that Jesus knew I was praying to him, and it would be fine.

The very second that my knees touched the kneeler, a bright light that looked like a flame of fire showed up right in front of my face. It was very large, as big as my entire head. Startled, I didn't open my eyes, but while the flame was there, from my left side I could feel the presence of someone, and then I felt a hug—a spiritual hug—not physically but spiritually. I was overwhelmed with the love I was receiving from a mother—not just any mother, but the most perfect mother, that didn't exist on this earth. I knew this mother was perfect, and the love I felt from her was overwhelming. The entire experience only lasted maybe ten seconds.

When it had ended, I turned to look for my husband to let him know that something had just happened to me. Completely overwhelmed with emotion, I described what took place. He said, "It sounds like you had a visitation!" I had no idea what he was talking about, but within seconds I heard the Lord say, "Remember, you asked me for a sign!"

Then I heard him said, "What if one of your older boys was engaged to be married . . . would it be okay with you if they respected their mother-in-law?"

I answered, "Of course, Lord, of course I would want them to respect her."

Then he said, "Would it be okay with you if they loved their mother-in-law?"

"Yes, of course, Lord—they must love her!"

He then asked, "Then how much more do you think I am okay with you respecting and loving my mother?" I was stunned at how simple it all was when he presented it like that to me!

And from that day on, I started praying the Rosary and I fell in love with the Blessed Mother. One day, I told my husband, "You don't understand—I'm so in love with her," and he just smiled and showed he understood. I would occasionally have an overwhelming scent of roses around me, but I didn't know that roses were associated with Our Blessed Mother until much later.

During this same time, I had an interesting conversation with my birth mother, Mary. She shared with me that she had named me Mary at birth. She also shared how her maternal grandmother had seventeen live births, and she told me about the Catholic history of her family. This was so amazing to me! The Lord was bringing everything full circle and made it clear that he was the one bringing me back into the Church. He reminded me that even at the time of my birth mother giving me up for adoption, she had requested that it be in a "not strict" Catholic home. I couldn't believe how the Lord was having so many things coming together at once. It was the most beautiful and overwhelming gift.

I made my general confession after being away from the Church for over twenty years. This was done by making an appointment with a priest, and the actual confession took me probably an hour and a half. When I was finished, the priest had many kind and loving things to say, and I felt so light—like I was literally reborn.

To my great surprise, confession has become my favorite sacrament, next to the Eucharist. I visit the sacrament very frequently, and I will tell you that there have been only a few times when I haven't shed tears. I always try to remember to ask the Lord to guide the priest in giving me any advice or suggestions to help me overcome anything I am struggling with. I always feel the love of God so strongly, sometimes as though he's literally standing next to me. The priest absolves our sins in Persona Christi. It is the power of Christ himself—Christ forgives the sin, not the priest in his own power.

In an article titled "Spiritual Warfare: Insights from Exorcists,"[9] Patti Maguire Armstrong lists some of her favorite quotes from exorcists:

- "When I walk into a room to do an exorcism, the devil doesn't see me, he sees Jesus Christ."
- "Confession is more powerful than an exorcism. One is a sacrament, and the other is a blessing. One confession is worth 100 exorcisms."
- "The devil wants to destroy the soul, and the soul is healed by confession. If people want to decrease the work of Satan, they should increase the use of confession."

The Sacraments of Reconciliation and the Holy Eucharist have been the instruments of my healing. The Lord knew all my wounds and scars, and he knew exactly how and when to gently lead me to healing and

---

9 Patti Maguire Armstrong, "Spiritual Warfare: Insights from Exorcists," February 7, 2017, SpiritualDirection.com, https://spiritualdirection. com/2017/02/07/spiritual-warfare-insights-from-exorcists.

the rebirth of my soul. I am not the same person I was before, and I am very happy to say that, but it is with great humility and nothing of my own self or power—it's all the workings of my Heavenly Father and Jesus Christ my savior. There have been times where I have literally felt like I was dying inside. Now I know that I was. I was unknowingly dying a little more and more to myself every time I went to confession, every time I received Holy Communion in a state of grace (or not received him out of humility and offered myself to the priest for a blessing). The Lord has been so kind and gracious in leading and guiding me.

The hardest part has been learning to love myself. Looking back at my younger weaker self, I often judged her weakness and her naivety. But just the other day, the Lord told me in adoration a great truth about this.

Journal Entry, November 9, 2022

Today I went to the adoration chapel for a quick prayer before an appointment. It's still on my heart, so much shame and guilt that after writing yesterday about the situations that led to me becoming pregnant. The Lord knew exactly what I could not articulate, and he asked me to have mercy on myself. He said, "That twenty-six-year-old young woman was filled with many wounds and scars, and she did the best she could on that day with all the circumstances." I couldn't believe it! My Lord was showing me and asking me to have mercy on the old me. Because I wasn't the same person that I am now, and I did the best I could in an overwhelming and confusing state. I'm still in shock; thank you, Lord, because I feel angry and embarrassed about that weak woman I was. And you have made it possible for me to have compassion for her! There is no love like yours!

This was a great time for Hans and me to put the Lord first, to let Jesus start to heal us, and to focus on our newfound faith. During this time, I kept getting a vision in my mind's eye of a priest laying his hands on my head and praying. I told my husband about these visions, and he said, "Then let's go to the church right now and have the priest pray." We drove to the parish, and Father M. without hesitation took me back to his office, where I described the time in our lives and everything that had transpired. He seemed to know exactly what to do. He told me not to be scared of the name, but that he was going to have me kneel down in front of the crucifix on the wall and he was going to be praying a prayer over me that was called a "minor exorcism prayer."

I knelt down, and he prayed over me in Latin, and when he was done, it felt like the weight of the whole world had been lifted off my shoulders. It was just another confirmation that my Heavenly Father was leading and guiding me every step of the way.

I continued to learn new things every day. The history and depth of the Catholic Church is incredible. Starting with St. Peter, you can trace the "keys of the kingdom" all the way to today's current pope. There are so many saints and doctors of the Church and the early Church Fathers; there is so much beauty and depth that we can never come to the end of all the beauty and richness in the Catholic Church. For Hans and me, every week was like Christmas as we dove deeper and deeper into the beauty of our Catholic faith.

The road the Lord had taken us down has been a mix of rugged roads with steep inclines, beautiful flowers covered with sharp thorns, and the most amazing, unimaginable truths around every turn. Soon he would take me into an even deeper more intimate relationship with him and his mother. I could never have imagined what would be waiting for me on the other side.

CHAPTER 11

Roses from Heaven

"Trials are nothing else but the forge that purifies the soul of all its Imperfections."

—St. Mary Magdalen de Pazzi

One day, we took Noah to one of his trumpet lessons. His instructor lived on a cul-de-sac, and both Hans and I would often go and just hang out in the truck together. This particular day, we went inside to pay his instructor and ended up talking for a few minutes. When we returned to the truck a few minutes later, there was a single, perfect, beautiful yellow rose on the outside of the truck right in the exact middle of where the dashboard was. It was obviously put there to get our attention. I turned to Hans and said, "Did you put a flower on the car?"

He chuckled and said, "No, did you?"

We both just smiled and then got out of the car to look around to see where the yellow rose might have come from, but there weren't many flowers around at all. We were surprised, and we both had a feeling that it was a miraculous happening. I told my husband that maybe it was from heaven, and maybe it was given to us because it was just days before his dad and stepmom would be arriving from Chile to be at our marriage blessing. I believe it was a little smile from heaven to encourage us and make us feel loved, and it did.

Soon enough we had taken all the steps and had our marriage blessed by the Church, and the ceremony was beautiful and special. It was very intimate, with just Noah and Hans' dad and stepmom there with us, and I will never forget it. Receiving Holy Communion during the ceremony was such a blessing, such a far cry from our first marriage. This was the church we had spent so much time in, and Jesus was there with us! My husband bought a beautiful picture of the Holy Family and had it framed and had them there as witnesses as well. We will never be without this special sacramental in our home.

Our marriage wasn't perfect, but now we had so much prayer and the sacraments backing us up. There were definite attacks and hurdles still to go through, but we were making progress, even if we couldn't tell sometimes. The tough days were farther and farther apart, and being at Mass, having access to confession, and able to have one-on-one counsel with priests when necessary has been incredibly powerful.

There were rifts in my family stemming from when things with my husband and I went sour in the previous years, and many of those relationships hadn't been healed. The enemy would use this on top of the previous wounds and continue to provoke hurt feelings and bad memories. I knew many of these family members truly loved me and had my best interests at heart, and I knew they just didn't understand why I wasn't giving up on my marriage. But the Lord had showed me directly what the outcome of such a decision would do to me and to my son, and that wasn't his will. Nonetheless, the enemy used the distance in those relationships; it was like throwing salt on open wounds. He was relentless in torturing me with the pain of the complex relationships that now ensued.

Thankfully, through these years, the graces I would receive from Jesus would be so overwhelming, as well as the love and comfort I felt as I regularly attended Mass and spent time in prayer and reading the Word. I experienced just as many highs as lows, but the lows are unfortunately easier to remember at times.

We eventually decided to leave Broomfield and move back to the area where we previously lived. We found a great Catholic middle school for Noah to attend. We quickly made Catholic friends and now belonged to a community of like-minded Catholics. I decided it was time to go back to hospice work, and Hans was doing hospice as well. This was not long after when the pandemic hit. The pandemic for us as homecare hospice nurses was at times stressful, but we were lucky we worked from home doing on-call appointments during that time. I learned to really depend on my relationship with God and listen to the Holy Spirit as much as possible as I was discerning different choices during this time. I have to say that Father God never let me down and gave me the most wonderful friends with strong faith to lean on when the pressure from all sides was overwhelming. My husband came through as a solid and calm support and was very supportive and caring during this challenging time. We ended up buying a home during the pandemic and were blessed with a fresh start.

Not too long after we had moved in and gotten settled, I started reading a book by Patricia Sandoval and Christine Watkins called *Transfigured*.[10] Patricia's testimony touched my heart; there were many similarities in our lives, from painful family disruptions and abandonment issues to our abortions. As I was lying in bed reading one evening, I came to the part where Patricia discusses being led to a

---

10 Christine Watkins and Patricia Sandoval, *Transfigured: Patricia Sandoval's Escape from Drugs, Homelessness, and the Back Doors of Planned Parenthood* (Sacramento, CA: Queen of Peace Media, 2017).

Rachel's Vineyard retreat for healing from abortion. As soon as she wrote of seeing a vision of her three children in Heaven, I was completely and utterly enveloped with overwhelming pain.

As I lay there sobbing, I was shocked at how much pain I was still feeling. And then, I clearly heard Jesus speak to me, in his most gentlemen-like voice. "I want you to go." I'm not going to lie, I was upset, and I didn't want to go to a retreat like this, and I told him. I said, "Why do you want me to go cry in front of a bunch of strangers for a weekend? How is that going to help me?"

I knew I wouldn't be able to say no to him, but I decided that if I had to go, I was going to insist on some conditions, because I knew there was a memorial service involved where women had the chance to name their babies. I had no idea how all these women seemed to know the sex of their babies; I had not been given any sort of vision of this at all. I explained to Jesus that if I were to go, he would need to reveal to me whether my baby was a boy or a girl so I could decide a name in private. I was very serious about this because I knew this retreat was going to be extremely hard and painful for me.

A few days later, I was home alone, sitting on the couch in peace and quiet. Suddenly I saw a vision of one of the days I had been with dad before he died. It was the time I had confessed my abortion to him, as he lovingly squeezed my hand to show his love and understanding as I cried. The Lord reminded me that, as I was sitting in a chair next to dad and telling him about the abortion, in that moment, I had had a vision—not in color, but in black and white—of a little girl wearing a dress with her hair in pigtails. The Lord said, "Remember?"

No, I thought, *I probably just made that up.* I decided to take myself back in time and tell Dad about the abortion again, this time envisioning a boy (a grandson) that my dad would be going to meet. Right away I knew: It didn't work! I immediately knew it was a granddaughter he would meet!

Then the Lord said, "See, you already knew."

I have a daughter! I thought. *I'm the mom of a girl, and she is in Heaven!* Then I decided to try and come up with a name. The whole idea of picking a name was just awkward; it just didn't feel right, and I gave up. The second I stopped trying, though, in my right ear I heard the softest, most feminine voice you could ever in your wildest dreams imagine, and I heard this angelic female voice just whisper one single word: "Rose."

I said out loud, "Rose!? Oh my goodness, that's the most beautiful name! I could never have picked that on my own!" At the time, I wasn't completely certain from whom the whisper came, although the Blessed Mother was high up on my list of possibilities, as well as my daughter herself.

As soon as I had this information, I felt more confident and comfortable, and I was certain I could get through the retreat. I made plans to attend, and as the days went on, I shared with my husband what had transpired. I just couldn't help imagining my sweet girl, Rose, in heaven. She would now be around nineteen years old. She would have fit perfectly in between her two youngest brothers; this was so painful for me to imagine. But now I was getting excited to go to the retreat that before I was just dreading.

When the retreat was just a week or two away, I received an email stating that the retreat had been canceled due to a very low number of women who had signed up. My heart just sank. First, I didn't want to go at all, and now I felt that if I had to wait five months for the next retreat, I would just burst open with all these new emotions that had been bubbling up. I called Eddie, the person who was going to be leading the retreat. I told her I couldn't imagine waiting for five more months. I explained how I really didn't even want to come at first, but Jesus had asked me to. After hearing my emotions in my voice, she told me that another woman had told her the same thing.

She asked me to please pray a Rosary and ask if another woman could join the group.

I prayed the Rosary, and within a few days I got word that our prayers had been answered and another woman was joining the retreat. Eddie then said that after hearing my voice, she realized the urgency and decided they would hold the retreat even if just one woman came. She also shared that hundreds of people were praying for us—this was so comforting.

Before I knew it, I was driving to Conifer, Colorado, to attend the weekend retreat. On the way, I was overwhelmed with emotions and a mix of nervousness and excitement all rolled into one. This new information—that I had a daughter in Heaven and her name was Rose—was just unbelievable. My heart was overflowing with so much love for her, and so much pain and anger at the abortion itself. I couldn't help but continue to go back to that day, the day I made that fateful decision that would change the trajectory of my life, and all of my children's lives. I would have done anything to bring her back, to go back and to make a different decision, but of course this wasn't an option. And I knew that I would have to live with this pain for the rest of my life.

The retreat was held in a huge, beautiful home in Conifer, Colorado. It was late September, and the weather was just lovely—not too hot and not too cold. As I walked in and met a few of the volunteers, I felt comfortable right away, and there was a peaceful ambiance. The first evening after all four women (and one of the women's husbands) had arrived, we had dinner and walked around the grounds. I was following a woman named Teresa, who was a little older than I was.

As they led us out of the home and outside, Eddie pointed to our left and said, "Over there is the memorial garden, and the rocks have the names of the babies on them." I was overcome with emotion and immediately started to cry. *How was I going to get through an entire weekend if already I cannot contain my emotions?* I thought. I instinctively grabbed Teresa's shoulder, and she turned around and faced me. I said, "I just cannot go over there," and everything started flowing out of me.

I told her how I didn't want to attend the retreat, but Jesus had asked me to, and how I told him I would only come if he made it known to me if my baby was a boy or a girl, and how he revealed to me that it was a girl. Then, when I told her about the moment when I was on the couch and was about to tell her the name the Lord had let be revealed to me, she started trembling and crying herself, but when I uttered the name Rose, she was barely able to get out through her sobs, and she said, "That's my baby's name!"

I gasped in unbelief. I didn't even pick this name myself, and it didn't seem like a very common girl name. Teresa went on, "This is not a coincidence!" We both stood there dumbfounded and then hugged and embraced each other. Our tears turned into smiles—we had this little secret that immediately had bonded us and let us know that there were surely heavenly beings at work here. The comfort and consolation that brought us was just so huge. That whole first evening and into the next day, every time we would look at each other, we would just shake our heads in unbelief and smile at each other.

On Saturday, the retreat started, and there was a lot of journaling and sharing. (It was a very personal experience, and I was thankful there was only four women there because the pain and the crying were intense.) Nothing could have prepared me for this; I can't imagine how many tissue boxes I went through. As soon as I would think, *surely there cannot be any tears left*, more would just flow. A priest was there to cover us in prayer, and we listened to different readings. I believed that God was at work, so I had to surrender to this process, as excruciatingly painful as it was.

Saturday evening at dinner, I sat between a younger woman named Ellie, who was pregnant with a baby girl, and Teresa. I had asked Ellie earlier in the day if she and her husband had any names picked out for her girl yet—thinking that if she said Rose, that would just be even more crazy and unbelievable, but she said they were considering some other names. As the dinner went on, I heard Ellie telling a story. (I was conversing with Teresa, so I didn't hear the whole story, but it sounded interesting, so I asked what she was saying.) She said, "Oh, I was saying that when my husband was my boyfriend before we were married, he was in the adoration chapel one day, and the Lord revealed to him that my baby was a girl, and her name was Rose."

I gasped in shock and disbelief and so did Teresa. We had our hands over our mouths and were so shocked that everyone at the table became silent and asked us, "What is going on? What is happening?"

We explained that both of our girls also were named Rose and that I also hadn't picked the name myself and relayed how it had been revealed to me. No one could believe it. Every person was just silent and shaking their heads in disbelief and awe. Then Eddie, who was sitting directly across from me, said, "In all the years I have done this retreat, not even TWO women have EVER had the same name for their babies!"

It was the most amazing miracle for all of us. We knew that our Heavenly Father and the Blessed Mother were involved. Everyone knew this was not an accident or a random coincidence; this was beyond any of those things. The love and amazement in the room was palpable. None of us could deny the feeling of being surrounded by God's presence, and we felt so blessed by this miracle that he knew would touch all our hearts in such an amazing and unforgettable way.

There is no way that I could put into mere words the rest of the weekend, but I will tell you that many graces just poured over us. On Sunday, we held the memorial service, where we each read a letter to our babies that we had written in adoration in front of the Blessed Sacrament. Although this is an extremely personal letter, I'm choosing to share it here so that the graces can be felt abundantly by anyone who reads it. I was the first one to read my letter to my daughter, Rose, at the service.

September 25, 2021

Dearest Rose,

I'm so very sorry that I didn't have the courage and strength to make a different decision that would have given you a chance at life on this earth. I've been grieving so long and missing you so much it hurts; it hurts so much I cannot put it into words. As you already know, it can be a little crazy down here. I'm at peace knowing that you are with Jesus, Mama Mary, and all the angels and saints, Papa and Grandma Matthews, Big Grandpa, and so many more. I have a strong feeling that you have been looking after me and your brothers for quite a while now. I pray that you will intercede and help watch over your brothers and guide them straight to Jesus. Please help them not to make many of the mistakes that you've had to see me make (and the painful repercussions of those decisions). I feel like somehow in their hearts they know about you. I know they will be so happy to know I have received healing and can let go of a lot of the grief. Not that it won't still hurt (the hole will be in my heart until I'm with you one day). I make you this promise: I will tell my story until the day I die, and your life and death will not be in vain. I know we've already saved at least one baby from abortion, and I pray there will be many more. Now that I have allowed myself to feel, grieve, and learn your name, I promise a day won't go by that I won't tell you how much I love you and do everything I can to be brave and stand up for life. I love you with an overflowing heart.

Love you so much!
Mama

When I finished reading my letter out loud, someone handed me a single yellow rose. My mind instantly went back to that day in the truck when the single yellow rose showed up. I intuitively knew they were connected. I also saw a black-and-white image of my daughter; the only detail was her very long, wavy hair. To convey the intense emotion she was feeling, in my mind's eye I saw her jumping up and down, the way someone who was very excited would do. I immediately knew that she was absolutely crazy about her brothers and wanted me to let them know about her and how much she loved them. I could feel how proud she was to have her brothers, and her love for them was immense.

The next morning, as we were all getting ready to leave, I started thinking of the yellow rose connection again. I asked one of the lovely women that ran the retreat, "Pam, I'm just curious, do you always hand out yellow roses?"

She said, "It's funny that you would ask. No, we never give out yellow roses—only red or white. I actually have no idea why we have yellow roses this time."

I just smiled to myself. So many graces . . . it was overwhelming.

As we were getting ready to leave, we all exchanged information so we could stay in touch with one another. I was having a conversation with one of the women, and for some strange reason the conversation went to the subject of bears. I explained that even though I had lived in Colorado my entire life, I had never seen a bear, only in the zoo.

As I made my way to my car, I called my husband to tell him I would be on my way home. He asked, "How was it?" and before I could answer him, as I turned onto a dirt road and was slowly driving, a huge brown bear came out of nowhere and started crossing the street right in front of me! I started yelling, "It's a bear—there's a big bear crossing the street in front of me!" My husband couldn't believe it, and we got off the phone so I concentrate on driving.

When I got home, Hans and Noah were so excited to see me, and I felt like I was on a natural high. The graces and healing that had transpired were immense and innumerable. The days and weeks that followed were filled with overwhelming joy, still mixed at times with periods of intense grieving.

One day, I sat down at my desk to write my daughter a letter—only what came out on paper was a letter to me from her. It was unbelievable, and it's the biggest gift. I've had to read this countless times when I'm tired of the pain or worn out from all the trials of this life. All I have to do is pick up my letter from Rose, and the tears begin, my heart cracks back open, and all the love comes flooding back in, and I make it through another day. This is the letter my daughter, Rose, wrote to me that day.

October 9, 2021

Dear Mama,

I forgive you; you know that. It hurts me so much to see you cry and see your pain. You're so sensitive, and I hope you know that's such a gift. Many people love you, despite what you may feel sometimes. I have witnessed and been a part of many of the miracles you have witnessed and have been a part of. I'm so proud of you for not ever quitting, for not ever giving up, no matter how dark, lonely, and bleak it all was. I've seen the attacks against you from the enemy, and as you already know, I have witnessed the Lord protecting you many times. I'm still here, I'm always here, and I've always been with you— you were just too sad to be able to recognize me. I'm so glad you were able to be brave and say yes to healing at the Rachel's Vineyard retreat. You're really on your way, Mama, and I'm so proud of you for always lifting up God, trusting Jesus, and standing up against abortion and other evils. You truly are a survivor of so many battles; you truly are a warrior like my brother says. Tell the world the truth unapologetically. Jesus and I have your back always, Love,

Rose

So, you can imagine how it feels when I hear, "It's your body and your choice" and hear people even advocating for killing babies at any stage. These precious lives are discarded in the trash, and pro-choice people lie to women and tell them that "it's not even a baby yet."

When a woman has a miscarriage and the baby was planned, everyone recognizes that it's a baby, and the mother and father grieve, sometimes extensively. These children are also in heaven and have the hope to one day be united with their parents. So how do we so easily believe the lie that abortion is different—that those "fetuses" are not yet human and somehow only become valuable and babies when they are wanted, when it's a convenient time? Well, I can guarantee you that it would have been much easier for me to keep this pain buried deep inside and to continue to ignore the truth of it.

Thankfully, Jesus was relentless in going after me, and he never gave up on me even when I had given up on myself. Father God was not going to let me go my entire life and not reveal the truth of my abortion to me—the truth that I killed my own child who was growing safely in my womb. The truth is that I was too scared and too afraid of the judgments of others, and I let those things rule my choices and let the fear control me. The truth is sometimes gut-wrenching and heartbreaking, but it's still the truth.

Being separated from my daughter is painful, but there is beauty at the end of the tunnel when we allow Christ in to the most ugly and darkest areas. He had so much compassion and mercy on me in all my lowest points, and this is an example of how he wouldn't let me go unhealed without my eyes fully opened to the full truth of what had happened.

As the weeks went on, I kept thinking about the two yellow roses I had received, and I felt strongly that they were given to me by the Blessed Mother. I wanted to know for sure, so I started googling yellow roses and the Blessed Mother. I found so much information about how the Blessed Mother is associated with roses, especially white roses, red roses, and yellow roses. According to Wikipedia.org:

> Mary is the most beautiful flower ever seen in the spiritual world. She is the Queen of spiritual flowers; and therefore, is called the Rose, for the rose is called of all flowers the most beautiful. But, moreover, she is the Mystical or Hidden Rose, for mystical means hidden. . . . Three colors are especially consecrated to Mary: white roses as symbols of her joys, red roses as emblems of her sufferings, and yellow (golden) roses as heralds of her glories. Roses have shown up

in some of the miraculous Marian apparitions that people worldwide have reported.

All of these facts made me even more sure, but I prayed that I would know for sure. A week or two later, I was at home alone one night while my husband was out on a hospice visit. When my husband came home, I could tell by his demeanor that something unusual had happened. He had trouble finding the words but said he had been called to a facility where the woman he was going to see was in her room at the end of a long hallway. He was surprised to see that she appeared to be in the transitioning phase of dying, since he didn't think anyone was aware of her decline, and she hadn't been on much medication. He realized she needed to be on morphine for her breathing and overall comfort, so he administered a dose.

As he sat with her for a few minutes, he felt led to pray with her. He noticed she was Catholic, and he was moved by her inner strength even though she seemed really fragile to him. He said he asked her to wait for a minute and then went out to his car and came back with his blessed rosary. He told her he would like to give it to her, and she leaned her head forward with as much strength as she could muster, and he put it over her head and around her neck. They prayed and talked for a few minutes, and then when he was getting ready to leave, she told him to get her a little decorated bottle. She told him it was blessed water from Lourdes, and she wanted him to take it. My husband was overwhelmed by the gesture and insisted that he couldn't take it. With all her strength, she said, "Take it!" My husband showed me the petite, antique-looking bottle. It was so beautiful!

Immediately I felt in my spirit that I should google one last time the Blessed Mother and yellow roses, and this time, a picture of the Blessed Mother dressed in white and blue at Lourdes immediately showed up on my phone—and at her feet were two single yellow roses. She found a way to answer my prayer and show me she had given me the roses. I was completely overwhelmed and amazed and my love and trust for the Blessed Mother grew all the more.

Soon, I would know a mother's love so perfect that it could only come from Heaven.

CHAPTER 12

Meet Your Mother

"And how does this happen to me, that the mother of my Lord should come to me?"

—Luke 1:43

After the Rachel's Vineyard retreat, I could tell I was different. A great amount of healing had taken place, and my daughter was so real to me that she felt palpable. I now had her to share in my joys and sorrows and could tell her I loved her and missed her often.

I took great comfort in knowing I would one day be reunited with her and also knowing that she was rooting for me. I sensed that it was important to her that I continue my efforts to protect life, especially the most vulnerable, and to spread God's love to as many as possible in however many days the Heavenly Father would give me while here on earth. She was all the motivation I would ever need, and she deserved nothing less than for me to use my time wisely, as she wasn't given the opportunity herself. I would make sure that she would not be forgotten. *Rose, my sweetest girl, Mama loves you so much! Thank you for all your love and prayers, sweetheart; I cannot wait to be with you and for you to be united with all your precious brothers and the others who know of you and already have so much love for you!*

As I continued to study the Catholic faith, attend Mass and adoration (daily if possible), the healing and the graces continued. At times I would be soaring high with the Holy Spirit, but just as surely, I would run into an obstacle and feel my heart and spirit shattered. It's impossible to put into words the highs and lows I experienced. The thing that helped me get by was always reminding myself that this, too, shall pass. The more I emerged from the storms, the more I could interpret things differently and the more perspective I had.

One evening, I was driving in heavy traffic to see a patient in a nursing home. The home was pretty crowded and a little dirty, and I realized when I got back to my car that I needed to use the restroom, but I didn't really want to go back into the building and gas stations were not an option for me. I wasn't sure I could make it the hour or so to get back home. I realized that my birth mother's house wouldn't be too far of a drive. If she was home, I could stop in there. We talked sporadically—not weekly or even monthly but on and off and around holidays or birthdays. I called her to see if she was home, and she answered immediately and said, "Of course, come by; I would love to see you." As I fought through the traffic, I thought about how cool it was that she still lived in the same house where she lived when she was pregnant with me over forty-six years ago.

I arrived and after using the restroom, my work phone was quiet for a bit and we got to sit and catch up for a while. Suddenly it just struck me. As I saw the way she looked at me and always made sure and expressed how much she loved me, I was overcome with emotions. She stood up to hug me, and I just melted in her arms, crying. I told her, "I just don't know what I would have done if I had never gotten to know you!" She just squeezed me and comforted me and listened thoughtfully as she always had.

Many times she would apologize, and I would reassure her that I was never mad at her—just thankful I had the opportunity to know her and to feel her love and be able to love her back. I was thankful for my adoptive family, and I loved my brothers and sister so much, even if those relationships weren't perfect, I had many great memories, and I especially loved having seven brothers growing up, since I was very much into doing whatever, they were doing, and I wouldn't have changed that for anything. I also loved my mom and dad (and stepparents) so much and couldn't imagine my life without them as my parents, and I could never thank them enough for adopting me and taking care of me when my birth mother wasn't able to.

I had also met a new half-brother, Rob, and two half-sisters, Jen and Kristin (Kristin was also given up for adoption), and I had formed some close bonds with them. My aunt Judy and I would also come to know each other, and she ended up being an invaluable encourager and supporter when I went through a very rough time. We were even able to attend Mass together, and that was wonderful. I also met Mary's father, "Grandpa George," my maternal grandfather, before he passed. He was a deaf mute from scarlet fever and communicated through sign language. I will never forget one day when we both were there with Mary. She was explaining to him who I was, and tears just started rolling down his kind face.

I see how similar my birthmother and I are in our personalities and how she has struggled so much with depression and anxiety, and I just don't know if I could have survived it struggling with those things so much myself. It's so amazing how the Lord knew the perfect and best fit for me, and I'm truly blessed and thankful to have all my siblings and parents and to have been covered with God's love and heavenly protection from birth.

The day after I had stopped by Mary's house, I decided to go to daily Mass at Queen of Peace in Aurora, Colorado— the same church Grandma and Papa Matthews had attended for many, many years. Grandma always came into my mind when I was there; I often would look to the area of pews where she usually sat. This day, during Mass, I was distracted. I silently in my head told the Lord, "I'm sorry, Lord, I don't know why I'm so distracted." I kept feeling my attention move to the left side of the church where I remembered there was a place to kneel and pray. I made a mental note that I would go over there after Mass. As soon as Mass was over and I finished praying, I walked over to the left side of the church, and when I saw it I remembered how incredibly beautiful it was; it's the deepest blue-colored stained glass of Our Lady of Guadalupe.

As I knelt to pray, she was there! I immediately was completely enveloped in the Blessed Mother's love and presence. Just as before with the flame, I was trembling and tears were pouring from my eyes. I said, "Mama, Mama, I love you so much!" The peace and love were so consuming and enveloping that my words and thoughts were not humanly controllable. I felt like a little girl, and I couldn't stop repeating, "Mama, Mama I love you—I love you so much, Mama!"

Then, intuitively I heard her speak. "Will you accept me as your ultimate mother?" she asked.

I quickly answered, "Of course, Mama, of course I will!"

"And will you let me help to heal all the wounds on your heart that were caused by your two earthy mothers?"

I then saw a black-and-white image of my heart with many cracks going through it. "Of course, Mama, of course," I said.

She then said, "And will you also let me help you to forgive anything that you might not have already forgiven from either of your two earthly mothers?"

"Of course, Mama, of course I will!"

And then she said (very nonchalantly, I might add, which made me giggle), "And keep reading that book!" The only book I had been reading around this time was *The Flame of Love of the Immaculate Heart of Mary: The Spiritual Diary* by Elizabeth Kindelmann. This "flame of love" is the same flame of love that had appeared to me five or six years previously after I had prayed for a sign from the Lord if it was okay to pray the Rosary. About four years later a piece of paper mysteriously had shown up on our coffee table—it had a picture of a flame and said something about the Flame of Love Movement.

As soon as I saw it, I yelled to my husband, "This paper—did you see this flame of love? This is what I saw! This is some type of movement, I guess." He said, "Yeah, I saw that." I couldn't believe it! I had no idea there was anything called The Flame of Love, and I now realized what I had seen in front of me years before at the Immaculate Heart of Mary Parish.

Now the Blessed Mother was asking me to finish reading Elizabeth Kindelmann's book, and I felt guilty that it was taking me so long. I felt the importance of obeying her.

When I first got the book, one morning I was on call for work and had woken up around 4:00 a.m. I got ready for work in case an early morning call came in and then grabbed the book and started reading it. Within minutes, I was overcome in my spirit. I thought, *How strange—she talks with Jesus and the Blessed Mother in such a similar way as me.* I felt a kinship with her and thought, *It's like we are soul sisters*, and that made me laugh. I was shocked at some of the things I was reading as I had felt similar things at times, and I might as well have been highlighting the entire book. Elizabeth had a lot of suffering in her life, but Jesus and the Blessed Mother explained to her that this is necessary for souls who are willing to participate in redemptive suffering with Jesus.

Here are a few excerpts[11]:

[Jesus] "My daughter, you will have to suffer much. I will give you no consolation that will tie you to the earth, but I will always give you My fortifying grace. Also, the power of the Holy Spirit will be with you. You must get rid of all that entices you to evil and live according to My pleasure. I can help you to find the right path. Immerse yourself in My teaching."

[Elizabeth] "In spite of all my efforts, O Lord, I see no progress in myself."

[Jesus] "Do not worry! Begin anew each day. Our Mother will help you, ask everything from her. She knows how to please me."

[Elizabeth] "Many times Jesus said to me: 'My daughter, renounce yourself. I keep insisting on this because you can only share in My work of Redemption

---

11 Excerpts taken from Elizabeth Kindlemann, *The Flame of Love of the Immaculate Heart of Mary: The Spiritual Diary* (Landsdowne, PA: The Flame of Love Movement, 2019), 15, 28, 99.

if you live united with Me at every moment. There must be no interruption.'"

[Mary] "With this Flame full of graces that I give you from my heart, ignite all the hearts in the entire country. Let this Flame go from heart to heart. This is the miracle of becoming the blaze whose dazzling light will blind Satan. This is the fire of love of union which I obtained from the heavenly Father through the merits of the wounds of my Divine Son. . . . Your merits, no matter how small they seem, will increase your graces. I entrust my Cause to just a few. After they are won over, a multitude will follow. Rejoice that you are one of the few. Unfortunately, even among the few, some reject me and cause pain to my motherly heart."

[Jesus] "Unite your sufferings totally with Mine. Then your merits will grow greatly and they will move My redemptive work ahead. Keep this great grace you received from Me in the depth of your soul. It is a special gift of God. He honors you, poor little soul. Can he give you anything more sublime? Learn from Me. I chose you because you are small and miserable. Never tired of suffering for Me."

[Mary] "My Flame of Love is so great that I can no longer keep it within me; it leaps out at you with explosive force. My love that is spreading will overcome the satanic hatred that contaminates the world so that the greatest number of souls is saved from damnation. I am confirming there has never been anything like this before. This is my greatest miracle ever I am accomplishing for all."

I encourage you to read the full *Spiritual Diary*. The Blessed Mother is obviously very involved with assisting us on this course toward heaven, and she obtains graces from her son. Who could deny her? Her love for all her children is so immense.

I doubt I will ever again feel the kind of love I experienced that day on this side of heaven, and I will never forget it. To be in Mary's holy, loving motherly protection is indescribable. But I can promise you that it is the most comforting love you can ever imagine! And she is just so loving!

Just as we adore and pray and look after our own children, the Blessed Mother is continually doing the same for all her earthly children, and she prays for us all and desires as many to be saved as possible. The Blessed Mother—along with Jesus, of course—wants nothing more than all of her beloved children to obtain Heaven. But that depends on us. We are all given free will; true love doesn't force itself upon anyone, and our Heavenly Father is no different. If you haven't already, open your heart to Jesus and Mother Mary who wait for you to come and rest in their loving arms and give your weary soul rest.

The Blessed Mother (Mama) has already healed my heart in so many ways, and it's like she did it instantaneously. Things that before caused me much pain and torment now cause little to no pain at all. I could never thank her enough for this healing, and I am forever grateful and full of an overflowing heart of love for her. There truly is no love like hers! She is the mother who comforted Our Lord, and now she comes to us with the same love she poured out on her son, and she waits for us with open arms. Run to your mother—she waits for you!

"Who am I, that the Mother of my Lord would come to me?" (Luke 1:43). I am humbled beyond words. Thank you, Mama, for your kindness, for loving your hurting and broken daughter, for healing my heart and inspiring me so! Please stay with me and never leave my side!

Love,
Your daughter

CHAPTER 13

A Whole New World

"I have been crucified with Christ and I no longer live, but Christ lives in me. The life I live in the body, I live by faith in the Son of God, who loved me and gave himself for me."

—Galatians 2:20, NIV

When the Lord asked me to write a book about adoption around fourteen years ago, I understood why. I knew I wasn't the only one who had subsequent questions and wounds from the adoption and relinquishment process, but I spent years stalling because I didn't want to hurt anyone's feelings in the process.

Then the Lord said one day, "If you can help one person by sharing your testimony, then all of your suffering will not be in vain." He made it clear that I shouldn't only write about the beautiful parts, but also all the dark and scary and ugly parts. I honestly didn't know how I could possibly share such personal things with this cold, dark, cruel world.

Of course, there are many amazing, loving, kind people in this world. I know this firsthand, because he has put many of them in my life. But there is so much evil and darkness, especially now.

The Lord set me free from the bondage of people-pleasing. Satan wants us to be enslaved by what other people think. God freed me of this; it was a process, for sure, but the amount of freedom that comes when you no longer care about others' opinions (especially if it has to do with how much you're praising or talking about the Lord) has been amazing.

I know I won't be standing in front of any human being on judgment day. But I will stand before the Almighty God of the Universe! This is where I plan to invest all my time and energy until that day comes. What better return on an investment do you know of? Fear is one of the biggest tools the enemy uses, because it keeps us in bondage, but humility is the greatest weapon against Satan there is. Make yourself as small interiorly as you can, and the closeness you will share with God is a by-product of that alone!

There would have been no do-overs, no second chances for me, without for the grace of God. My life wouldn't have been saved many times over. Without his great love and mercy on my soul, I wouldn't be here right now. I wish to convey to you in the strongest way possible that it doesn't matter what you have done, or what you are currently doing. If there is air in your lungs as you read these words, you still have time.

God created you with a purpose and a plan, and he wants nothing more than for you to complete that plan and live this life as fully as possible so your eternity will be spent with him in Heaven.

If you haven't fully surrendered to Our Heavenly Father and/or the Blessed Mother, please do not delay. I am writing this with great urgency in my heart. I see the world lying to so many souls; even some church leaders will lie to spare people's feelings. Many church members are living in immoral, sinful lives, and they will have to answer to God for that.

If you know that someone is living in sin that could separate that person from God for eternity, and you don't feel like having an awkward conversation with them, so you choose to ignore it and let them think it wasn't that big of a deal, then you don't really love that person. If you love someone, and you see them about to walk off a cliff, you tell them—you warn them.

I pray that if you are living in sin, if you are struggling with sin, you will seek prayer. I pray you will continually get on your knees and ask the Lord for forgiveness. The

Sacrament of Reconciliation will help break the chains of the enemy. The enemy wants nothing more than to continue to convince you that he doesn't exist. It's a lie—he exists. I have felt what it feels like to have the enemy of our souls right next to me.

The Lord, in his goodness and mercy, has shown me firsthand how real Satan is. I am not a super brave or courageous person; I wish I was. To be that close to the enemy of our souls is completely and absolutely terrifying. He wants to kill you, to have you continue to numb your pain, and to continue to live in bondage to that sin.

You might think, *Hey, there's always tomorrow.* Well, there is always tomorrow . . . until there's not. Right now, it's not too late. I beg you to not wait, do not chance your eternal salvation for temporal comforts or fake accolades and believe that you have all the time in the world. Do not believe the cowards who are going around saying everything is permissible. They either don't know of hell or they don't believe in it; either way, they are sadly mistaken. We are living in the end times. Jesus is coming back soon, and he will judge the living and the dead. One more time, Jesus is coming back to judge the living and the dead (whether you believe this or not), and he is trying to warn you, because he LOVES you!

Christians have been given many prophetic words and warnings. The most urgent one that I know of right now is in a book written by Christine Watkins called *The Warning: Testimonies and Prophecies of the Illumination of Conscience*.[12] These are people who have experienced personally the coming judgments of our God. It describes a time coming soon when time will stand still and every person on earth will experience seeing all of their sins through their entire lives through God's eyes. They say it will be extremely painful and shocking at the same time, and people will know where they would go if they were to die that day. It is said that some will even die of shock or because their grief and pain will be so great. The coming "three days of darkness" has been foretold by many, and many great saints and mystics have said they believe it will happen including Padre Pio and Saint John Paul II.

I have been told that I experienced a "mini" version of this. Well, if the ten to fifteen seconds of hell that the Lord let me experience (what I believe to be the highest level of hell) is any help to you, please, I am telling you that those mere seconds of my life were unbearable, and if the Lord hadn't shortened it, I would surely have had a stroke or heart attack from the certain fear and terror of not

---

12 Christine Watkins, *The Warning: Testimonies and Prophecies of the Illumination of Conscience* (Sacramento, CA: Queen of Peace Media, 2019).

knowing if I was going to be in that everlasting ongoing darkness forever. It was completely devoid of God, and I understood that if I were to die in that instant, hell is where I would go. Not because God didn't still love me or not want me anymore, but because he is a just and holy God, and it is not in his nature to go against the laws of his universe already set into motion. He has made the ways in which we are to conduct our lives clear, and it's up to us where we end up. You see, we don't understand; we think hell is reserved for the vilest, most disgusting, most unrepentant child-molesting monsters, and there *is* a place in hell for them, if they don't repent. But there are other places in hell for those of us who did believe in God—some like me, who never stopped loving God, who never doubted him, and who did many good things in his name but committed a mortal sin, while he was trying to warn me and get my attention, knowing fully well he wasn't okay with it, even for a short time.

Or maybe you say, "Well, I'm a good person and I don't sin, so I should be fine." Let me tell you, the God of the Universe is HOLY. Things we don't even recognize as sins are often great offenses to him. Your eternal salvation is not something about which you can just flip a coin. The Bible says that no one knows the time or the hour, but it provides signs so God's people will know when it's near.

All the signs are here. Now is the time to think about the hard questions.

One of the things I had to work on was to be completely honest with myself and ask the Lord if there was anyone I hadn't forgiven. After I prayed that prayer, I had a dream about a family member several times in the course of a week. I also had a vision of a family member during Mass after receiving Holy Communion; in my vision, he was a toddler-aged boy. The Lord showed me that this person, too, had wounds and had been hurt by some of the same things I experienced. I saw golden rays coming down from Jesus like in the Divine Mercy image, and I was able to feel the love that God the Father had for this family member.

The love I felt for this person was so overwhelming that I was shaking and crying. The Lord had never let me feel his love for another person like this before. It completely renewed me and healed a fractured place in the relationship. I never ever had stopped loving this person, but I had been hurt by some of their decisions. My love for this person was so renewed, and I instantly had no more unforgiveness in my heart for him. God reminded me how much he loved this person, and he showed me how his wounds came from the enemy, just like mine had.

This experience helped me forgive many people, and it has helped me continue to choose love and work through healing whenever negative emotions or bitterness comes up. God knows just how to reach us—it's amazing. Now, every time someone comes into my mind, especially if it's a bad memory, I make sure to pray for that person. It's hard to pray for someone who has hurt you, but when you become so consumed by and filled with God's love and mercy that you find it easy to pray for them, you know you're on the right path.

In other times God has shown me certain people that I had offended, and in a couple situations he told me specific things I should do to make amends. These were great graces, and I cannot begin to speak to all of them, only to say that the ocean of God's love and mercy are never ending, and I pray that you, too, continue to seek his truths and great mercies.

As the years went on after returning to Catholic Church, I've had this great, colorful mix of the highest highs and the lowest lows. I must admit, I'm not a very good sufferer—I'm horrible at it. It takes me a long time to learn certain lessons and understand the complexities of suffering, looking through the lens of redemptive suffering.

I think the great irony of my life and the biggest blessing is that my strongest and most secure relationship with the Lord has now taken root and is most secure after so much pain, failings, and sufferings. God the Father always knew my deep love for him and my intentions to try and do the best I could at any given time. I now have a faith so deep and rich I could never adequately describe it in mere words, but the deeper my suffering, the higher I have soared. Suffering is a grace that catapults you to God. If I died today, I would pray for the courage, but I would have hope that with Jesus holding my hand, I would make it!

There have been days that I have longed for Heaven like never before. On one of these days, my husband and I had a terrible argument, and we were both tired and very stressed. I had been going to Mass and/or adoration daily, yet just felt so far from my Lord. I decided to drive to St. Thomas More, and while I was there at the church, I paid a visit to the cove, a little enclave filled with many first-class relics and dozens of pictures of different saints. This is my journal entry from that day, written sometime at the end of August 2022:

Today I was very, very down. I felt defeated and like I needed more strength. I drove to the cove at St. Thomas More parish hoping, praying for some reprieve. I felt guilty after speaking to a particularly stern priest who said we shouldn't "expect" or "ask" Jesus for "signs or consolations." Anyway, I knew

Jesus knows my heart, and I also knew that he already knew my fragility right now and all the attacks from the enemy I'm going through. I prayed and assured Jesus that I did not expect anything ever from him or Mama Mary but shared my deep sorrow that I was carrying. I prayed only for strength and help to lift my spirits if he saw fit, and I told him how hard and heavy my spirit has felt the past week.

As soon as I stepped through the doorway of the cove, I felt Mama's presence at my left side where the Our Lady of Guadalupe picture hung. Her presence was so strong that I dropped to my knees, trembling and crying. I told her again and again how much I loved her, and I placed my hand on her feet. I was in disbelief that she was there; I was sure after the first time that I was never going to experience her love like this again. I explained to my husband how very hard it was after she first showed up to me. I was so incredibly thankful and humbled by her first visit to me, but it made me so incredibly sad and miss her so very much.

Daily, I longed to feel her love and presence. Wherever I was, if I passed by a photograph or statue of Mary, an automatic response would come out of me, and I felt like a child calling for her. I would say

"Mama! Mama!" as though trying to call her to me, and then when she wasn't there, I would express my love for her and keep walking. I told my husband, 'I understand that I probably won't ever get to feel her around me again, and I would never expect it, but at the same time, I do inevitably miss her so much and can't put it into words how much I miss her now.' And I would tear up thinking back to being in her presence and the amount of love and peace was obviously not of this world, and I would not be able to describe it adequately with human words.

But now, she was here again. I knew intuitively that she knew how much I was suffering—she was acutely aware—and that made me cry even more. I was shocked to hear myself say, "Just take me with you, Mama!" through the tears streaming down my face. I was so comforted by her presence; it was in the starkest contrast to this cold world, and while I certainly didn't want to leave my children or husband, in that moment that was what came out.

I moved to one of the kneelers for more privacy and continued to cry and pray. I found myself turning before Jesus in the Divine Mercy Image and began again pleading my case. "Please, Jesus, please! You know I'm not this strong; you KNOW I'm not this strong! Please, take me with you! I need to go with you; this is too hard, let me go with you!"

Before I knew it, I was off the kneeler and on the floor again, just overwhelmed with the knowing that soon their strong, loving presence would be gone, and I would once again be left alone. I got back up on the kneeler and bowed my head in prayer as I knew I had to let go and continue until it was my time. A peace came over me and calmed my heart and spirit. I knew that I was suffering greatly, but before this experience, even I didn't realize how much.

I was incredibly in awe and very touched. I stayed in the cove for a while afterward and asked any of the saints who felt they could help or assist me in any way to please do so, and told them how grateful I would be. I was acutely aware of their witness and how they were rooting me on, and I felt a sense of kinship knowing that they also saw me and cared for me. I then went to the gift shop and bought a beautiful Our Lady of Guadalupe image for my husband and our home. Deacon George was there and blessed it for me with a beautiful prayer.

As I returned home, I felt a new strength within me, and I was so thankful for all the heavenly love and support. I often ponder this great love I have for the Blessed Mother and think that if anyone had told me I would one day have this great love for her, I never would have believed it. *Thank you, Mama and Jesus, I will continue the best I can until you say. I'm so thankful that I know you are protecting my boys and keeping them safe, and I love you so much.*

Following this most miraculous visitation in the cove, the feeling of that love and peace definitely was a comforting balm for my heart and soul. But there were things in my life that I was still struggling with, and some of them had to do with my marriage. Many years had gone by, and we had gone leaps and bounds in our relationship in so many ways. But the enemy was relentless, using either hurtful memories or anything else he could to cause an argument or division between us.

One night, we had gone to an evening Mass at Our Lady of Lourdes Parish in Denver. They have a 6:00 p.m. Mass with confession beforehand, and often it was the best fit for all of our different schedules. As I sat in one of the front left pews before confession, my attention kept being drawn to the left side of the altar. I wasn't wearing my glasses, but I knew to the right was the Blessed Mother, and I couldn't tell if it was Jesus or St. Joseph on the left, but I felt an overwhelming pull to go up and pray.

In my mind's eye, I saw an image as though someone was gesturing me to come closer. I had the strongest feeling that it was St. Joseph, and that was different for me because although I had great respect and love and admiration for St. Joseph, I seemed to always be focused on Mama and Jesus. I would sometimes forget to pray to him, and then I would find a random prayer card with him on it and then would remember and pray to him.

I asked my son, who was sitting next to me, "See that statue over there? Is it St. Joseph, or Jesus?" He was used to this sort of thing and immediately said, "St. Joseph." I was so surprised and happy, and immediately I felt completely drawn up out of my seat and went and prayed before him. It gave me such a chuckle, and I was so honored that he had even considered me at all.

Well, after that it started. Whenever I would find myself in front of a St. Joseph statue or picture, I was drawn to him and felt like I wanted to kneel and pray in front of him. I felt his fatherly protection and love in a truly palpable way. Sometimes I felt bad for not giving the Blessed Mother as much attention, but I assumed she knew something was going on. Well, then she gave me a hint and showed me in my mind's eye a picture with both of her hands covering the sides of my head as she gently turned my gaze toward St. Joseph. She showed me that she herself was leading me to her holy spouse, St. Joseph.

Not long after this, I was at the kitchen table one evening and decided to watch a new episode of *The Journey Home*. As I was watching the show on and off, mostly just listening, someone mentioned something about St. Joseph, and I found myself immediately sprinting towards the television. Afterward, I was on the phone with my friend Eileen and told her I felt I was supposed to do the Consecration to St. Joseph. We had discussed this before, but now there was this real urgency for me to complete it.

A couple of days later, I found a book written by Father Donald Calloway, *Consecration to St. Joseph: the Wonders of Our Spiritual Father*. My husband, son, and I decided we should all do it together as a family. After that, everything was different. There was something that only St. Joseph could do for my family—he was the missing piece! The protection he gave me was immense, and I immediately was completely in love with him, too, just like with Mama. This was the most special thing, and I cannot recommend the Consecration to St. Joseph enough. The Holy Family is our most amazing model and most holy protection we can get while here on earth. St. Joseph, you have completed my family! I love you!

For once in my life, I now get to be brave and stand up for my number-one supporter and Savior, my Lord Jesus Christ. He prepared my heart and my spirit to let go of all this world has to offer, and he made the evil easy to see. He promised me that even if everyone in my life abandoned me, HE would always be there and would never leave me or forsake me! He is the kindest, bravest, most sincere, most honest, most loving, and most forgiving Lord, and his sense of humor is amazing! He is my great caretaker, my all-time greatest love, and I owe him everything! When he speaks to me, I'm humbled and melt with a heart of burning love and longing for him.

> Father God, it's amazing how you work. I see through this writing process how I've been forced to start loving myself and having grace and mercy for myself. It's been so painful and hard at times to write, and other times so easy! Your love is so all-encompassing and overwhelming—I can't breathe without your unwavering love! Thank you for not ever giving up on me and for being the most patient and kindest gentleman that has ever walked this earth.
>
> Until I get to be with you, please help me to be in your will and to stay strong and hopeful, knowing you are always there and will never leave me. Thank

you so much to all my amazing friends who make my life complete and who understand me; I can never repay all of you for your countless prayers for me and my family, but God will most surely reward you! And thank you for the most beautiful, kind and caring children a mama could ever dream of. Please continue to watch after us all, and lead and guide us in your ways you would have us all go.

Love,
Your daughter

CHAPTER 14

Broken Glass

"To suffer means to become particularly susceptible, particularly open to the workings of the salvific powers of God, offered to humanity in Christ. In him God has confirmed his desire to act especially through suffering, which is man's weakness and emptying of self, and he wishes to make his power known precisely in this weakness and emptying of self."

—St. John Paul II, Salvifici Doloris

Right as I thought my journey of suffering, healing, and being refined by fire was coming to an end (as far as this particular journey of sharing my story), the Lord gave me one more chapter that I wasn't expecting. Although I wasn't planning on it, I experienced some of the most beautiful emotions mixed with another wave of overwhelmingly painful emotions and some more grieving. The pain is so bittersweet when the Lord weaves it together with just enough glimpses of him walking through it all right next to us. And just when we are sure we cannot bear any more of it, he proves us wrong by giving us beautiful, intricate little surprises that he knows will be just enough to sustain us and help carry us through the pain of that day, week, or month.

Adoption is an extremely complicated and multifaceted situation for everyone involved.

I knew my adoption had affected me greatly, despite having a loving and caring family. In an article titled "Relinquishment Trauma: The Forgotten Trauma"[13] the author states, "When relinquishment trauma occurs, it happens due to an infant's traumatic experience after the separation from their mother and the loss of the familiar." She goes on to say:

> Relinquishment trauma is one type of adoption trauma. Additional traumatic adoption events adoptees may experience include an absence of information about birth family creating genealogical bewilderment", and others. There are trauma wounds when a birth mother gives an infant away. Experts admit that a baby knows when they are being taken care of by strangers.

---

13 Marie Dolfi, "Relinquishment Trauma: The Forgotten Trauma," https// mariedolfi.com/adoption-resource/relinquishment-trauma-the forgotten-trauma/.

Many (not all) of us adoptees have had abandonment issues and trouble with trusting and bonding at times. We question why we are here if we were never really meant to be; we often question our identity and our place in this world. More than fifteen years ago, when I first heard the Lord ask me to write a book on adoption, he made it crystal clear, saying, "You will not be fully healed until you write this book." But through this process, I never imagined this journey would lead me back to the Catholic Church. Yes, I've stated this several times already—hence, it shows how shocked I still am.

The Lord has healed my brokenness and wounds through the sacraments of receiving the Most Holy Eucharist and going to very frequent confession. These two things have literally changed my life; they changed the fabric of my very being. They have broken me down, refined me with fire, caused me die to myself, and then, through their miraculous healing powers, began picking me up and putting me back together as a stronger, more confident, and healed woman who knows her identity came from God. As he let Christ journey with me down the jagged, sometimes treacherous road, I thank God he was there holding my hand along the way. He then introduced me personally to the Blessed Mother (Mama) and my spiritual father (St. Joseph), making it as though

the entire Holy Family had adopted me into their very
own family! It's the most indescribable love! Then, he
gave me the ending of this book, reminding me that HE
is the author of ALL of our stories! May God Bless you
always!

April 23, 2023, The Third Sunday of Easter; confession
and Mass at Our Lady of Lourdes

I was very emotional at Mass contemplating two
completely different situations that the Lord seemed
to be simultaneously messaging me and unveiling the
different perplexities and details to me strand by strand.
After receiving Most Holy Communion, I started to weep
as privately as possible. The union with Christ in that
moment has proved to be the most powerful and healing
and miraculous mystery. As I tried to calm myself down,
I heard the Lord ask me, "Was it worth it?" I opened
my ears, trying to fix my attention solely on Him, then
I heard him say, "Would you do it again? I intuitively
knew that he was talking about my entire life and any
and all suffering I had endured to that point. Of course,
he already knew what my heart was aching about. He
then made it profoundly clear. He said, "Would you do
it all again? Would you endure all the pain and suffering
again if you knew you would get to experience this close

intimate union with ME?" Immediately all the beautiful and glorious blessings and love and graces overflowed in my mind and the suffering dimmed. I quickly answered him saying, "Of course, Lord! Of course! A hundred times over I would!"

And that was it—in that one moment, he had taken all the pain and suffering and reduced it to the small minuteness of what it all really was, while overflowing my heart and soul with the innate knowing of his glorious love for me.

My Lord, I don't deserve your love!

April 29, 2023

Last night, as I was driving home many miles from a visit, I was praying for anyone and everyone who came into my mind. Earlier in the day I went to confession and Mass at Risen Christ Parish, knowing I would be working and most likely too tired to go on Sunday. I was very early for confession and was alone in the church. There was only one soul praying up at the front, and the lights were dimmed. I was praying a novena prayer and noticed that a man dressed in black had come in and also sat down. When I was done praying, I realized this young man had gotten into the confession line, so I decided I would too. He immediately looked over at me and said, "Oh, you were here first; please go ahead of me." I politely declined as I usually take a minute to prepare, and I didn't need to rush. He continued to make sure and then offered that he would save my spot if I wanted to sit down.

I said, "Oh, thanks so much, but I'm okay, really." His face was so beautiful, and he had this amazing light illuminating from his youthful brown eyes. He just overflowed with love and what appeared to be the Holy Spirit. I quietly asked him if he was a seminarian, and he said with a big smile, "Oh, no, not yet. I've basically been living like a monk for two years during the discernment process." I smiled, still overcome with the kindness and love I felt radiating from him. His presence and smile alone had touched a place deep in my heart.

Of course, my Heavenly Father knew everything that I had been contemplating, and it was all very heavy stuff. I felt such a draw to this young man in my spirit, like I had never experienced before. He felt holy and pure. He told me his name, and we got into a conversation about the private things I had been going through, and I asked if he would be so kind to keep my family in his prayers. He immediately said he would and handed me his small notebook and pen so I could include the name of specific family members and prayer intentions. He then offered up some personal information about things he and his family had gone through, and it was very personally related to mine. He told me he specifically had a heart to pray for the actual prayer intentions I wrote down because of something similar in his family. I was shocked, but at the same time not too much because I could feel this was Divine Intervention.

Suddenly, his face looked very serious, like he had been given private information, and he said in a somber, gentle tone, "Would it be okay if I prayed over you?" Are you kidding me, Lord? I was overcome with emotion and had such a full heart. I closed my eyes and bowed my head while he prayed. The tears immediately were streaming down my face more and more with every word he said. I realized as he was praying that it seemed as if the Lord wasn't letting me recall exactly what he was saying. I was trying so hard to pay attention, but I couldn't. All I can remember is that it seemed like he had given me a compliment, which was so humbling and touching and I could remember just a few words: *Lord . . . protect . . . heal . . . comfort*, to the best of my memory. As we parted ways, I wondered if I would ever see him again. Would he become a priest? I told him I was so thankful to have met him, and he said, "Me too." I said, "We need more holy priests so badly," not meaning in the slightest way to put any pressure on him, and he smiled so kindly and gently and said, "We do; we really do." I was so thankful for the godly intimacy we shared that can only happen when the Holy Spirit is fully present.

As I went on to confession and Mass, I was overcome with a mix of emotions and started to cry again. I was so overwhelmed by the Gospel message, and my heart was overflowing with love for my Lord as usual. Suddenly, my mind returned to a recent situation that had come up in my life. Kind of out of the blue, a family member asked me if I had known who my birth father was. I said, "No, I don't know who he is; he doesn't even know I exist."

This ended up opening a new part of my adoption journey that I didn't think was ever going to come into play. It was the one area of my life that I had pretty much decided would never be known to me. When this family member told me of a nonprofit organization that reunites birth families that are separated, my mind went back to that weird place of not knowing and how it felt like there was half of me out there (my biological father) that I knew nothing about. I decided that as I was almost done writing my testimony, which contained a lot of my adoption story, it could be the last missing piece I never knew about and possibly needed healing from.

I decided to take a chance—and truthfully, I didn't pray a lot about this first. I was extremely surprised when I received a call the very next evening from a very nice man who had already begun searching for this man who was possibly out there and had no idea I existed. I was extremely emotional and shocked at how much emotion this was stirring up in my soul. There were several times when I had second thoughts about whether this was something I really needed to do.

I had been given an amazing, adoptive dad, with whom, though now in Heaven, the bond is, if anything, even stronger. I had gotten peace with my birth mother, and just as important (or even more important), she had received her final peace and closure knowing I was okay, and she was then able to fully heal. I knew I had the love and special protection of St. Joseph, and somewhere down deep in my soul, I felt God the Father trying to get my attention. It's hard to explain; I felt like he was warning me that this was something that could bring up difficult emotions for me. The nice man doing the search kept reassuring me and saying, "I think you're thinking too much into this; it's okay." Before I knew it, he had narrowed down my biological father to one of two brothers. He said, "This is it—this has to be it!"

The shock and emotion that ran through my veins was overwhelming. I looked at the picture of the one with the higher probability because of public records at the time. I kept going back to this man's face over and over. Was it just me, or would anyone else see this? In this man's face, especially in his eyes, I saw *my* eyes. I saw some features that resembled my sons. I was shocked. I had never been able to look into another person's face and see part of myself. As I asked a couple people, they immediately said, "Oh, yes definitely," or "Absolutely! You're definitely related."

Well, eventually the journey led me to talk with a young man I believe to be my half-brother. I'm going to keep the rest of this private for the sake of the newness and all the parties involved, but I will share that when this incredible human being with an amazing heart saw my picture, he told me that he said to himself, *That's my father's face.* Well, unbeknownst to him, I had just about come to the end of this healing journey, and the title of my book that I had been writing for many, many years, was titled *The Face in the Mirror.* I couldn't believe my ears! I had always looked in the mirror and thought, *Where did I come from? Who do I look like?* Now this amazing young man had just brought this peace and love and sense of completeness to my heart with that one sentence.

But the most amazing thing of all was how the Lord spoke to me at Mass and brought to my mind and attention all the instances of men, women, and children, who for many numerous reasons won't ever get to even glance at the face of a close family member and see their face in theirs. Or won't hear of certain personality similarities, etc. And this is where it gets hard, and this is whom I want to speak to right now. This is who my Heavenly Father spoke to me about this night. He reminded me that HE was the author of my story and of ALL of our stories.

The hardest part for us to understand in our humanness is why certain things happen to us, and why some of us feel so broken and wounded. God the Father reminded me that he is my Ultimate Father, and he is the Ultimate Father of us all. He said, "Many times we don't feel a perfect love from our earthly mothers and fathers because they are only human beings, and they are often times broken and hurting still themselves." He reminded me that there is so much brokenness in this world, with fractured relationships, people struggling with different addictions, men, women, and children suffering from cancer or other illnesses, and so on. Our Heavenly Father calls us into this most intimate relationship (the ONLY relationship where we can experience GOD Intimacy) that completely triumphs everything else.

My Heavenly Father has saved me in every way a person can be saved—literally, physically, emotionally, spiritually, every way! When all this came to me, it was right before Mass started on April 29, 2023. Then I heard the First Reading for the Fourth Sunday of Easter:

"Then Peter stood up with the Eleven, raised his voice, and proclaimed to them, "You who are Jews, indeed all of you staying in Jerusalem. Let this be known to you, and listen to my words. Therefore let the whole house of Israel know for certain that God has made him both Lord and Messiah, this Jesus whom you crucified." Now when they heard this, they were cut to the heart, and they asked Peter and the other apostles, "What are we to do, my brothers?" Peter [said] to them, "Repent and be baptized, every one of you, in the name of Jesus Christ for the forgiveness of your sins; and you will receive the gift of the Holy Spirit. For the promise is made to you and to your children and to all those far off, whomever the Lord our God will call. He testified with many other arguments, and was exhorting them, "Save yourselves from this corrupt generation." Those who accepted his message were baptized, and about three thousand persons were added that day. (Acts 2:14, 36-41)

I was deeply moved at Mass, and then during the night, I had to make a long drive for a hospice visit. I decided to spend the drive completely in prayer. On the way home from the visit, I was overwhelmed by a strong message . . .

In my heart and spirit I was told that we only have one life here on earth, and when we're gone (after we die), we will have further knowledge of God's reasons and ways. I was overcome with the strong knowing that we will actually wish we would have realized the great blessing of suffering! In my spirit, I felt people yearning to be able to come back to earth and suffer more for our great God. Souls actually long to suffer greatly and wish they had realized it sooner while here on earth. Here on earth, we can reject the suffering, or we can trust God that in the suffering we are receiving great gifts and blessings.

It's hard to completely understand in the here and now, but we know the Bible talks about redemptive suffering. An article in the *National Catholic Register* begins with a quote from St. John Paul II: "In bringing about the Redemption through suffering, Christ raised human suffering to the level of the Redemption, thus each man, in his sufferings, can also become a sharer in the redemptive suffering of Christ."[14] He showed me the great beauty and

---

14 Dave Armstrong, "The Bible Says Your Suffering Can Help Save Others," February 1, 2019, *National Catholic Register*, https://www.ncregister.com/blog/the-bible-says-your-suffering-can-help-save-others#:~:text=2%20Corinthians%201%3A6%2D7,same%20sufferings%20that%20we%20suffer.

gift that suffering can be when we are walking through it with him. Faced with great trials and sufferings, we can actually still experience a deep, deep peace and love, when we unite it to our Heavenly Father and trust him through the suffering. He will never leave you or forsake you, he is always there with us, even when we can't feel him, he is there, and we can trust that he will not waste one single ounce of our suffering.

Now, onward to the Cross! Lord, continue to crucify me until it is no longer I who live, but only you who lives in me!

CHAPTER 15

Intimate Talks with God

"God speaks in the silence of the heart. Listening is the beginning of prayer."

—St. Teresa of Calcutta

I hope you have been encouraged when reading my story and reminded of how much God loves you. To bring this book to a close, here are some excerpts from my journal. May you draw close to Our Lord, Mother Mary, St. Joseph, and all the angels and saints as you continue your own faith journey!

Monday, February 27, 2017

Today is the ninth consecutive day of attending Mass or adoration. Lord, my soul is so overwhelmed. I'm completely at peace and could not need or want for anything more. I'm in disbelief, Father, of the way you have gotten me through this time. It's unbelievable what you have brough me through and how far I have come. Going to Mass or adoration daily has changed my life, and now, as you continue to relay all of these truths to me, after Mass I went to Father M. and gave him my praise report. Lord, how humbled I am that you could love me this much! You're so amazing; my love affair with you I could never put into words. If I never live past this day, I have been forever blessed beyond words. God bless my family, friends and all your people! This love flowing from me is indescribable! Oh, how I'm blessed! Father, thank you for holding all of my children in the palm of your hand; never let them go! For beyond you, Lord, there is nothing more important than my children's safety and the assurance of them spending eternity with you!

Tuesday, March 7, 2017

There is nothing in the world like a mother's love. Even Jesus felt the love of his precious mother, Mary. Praying the Rosary is Jesus wanting us to have a way to tap into our Blessed Mother's love for all of us. Jesus, tonight thank you so much for showing me why you would have us pray to your mother you share with us. The Blessed Mother is our mother also—how beautiful and yet another gift you've given us. Oh Jesus, how I love you. Oh Jesus, how I long for you! Thank you for sharing your Blessed Mother with me. You knew I would need her comfort, love, mercy, and graces . . . and most of all, her prayers. Please continue to speak to my heart, Jesus, and stay close to me.

March 13, 2017

I feel like I'm at a crossroad or about to cross a bridge. Jesus has been preparing my heart to finally start healing after so much suffering and struggling in my life. To feel every emotion so deeply is both a blessing and a curse. Grandma Matthews was always worried about me. I wonder if she is ever around me—oh, I miss my dad and grandma so much. It's hard to imagine heaven and being reunited with them both, and with my baby. As much as I regret my abortion, I'm so thankful that one day we will be reunited.

March 15, 2017

Today was good—not all good, but I feel the peace that only comes from you, Jesus. I'm thankful for my necklace blessed by the priest. It's like I have all these signs and this peace in my spirit about the Catholic Church. Yes, there has been great evil in the Church, but that doesn't take away from the fact of the beauty and truth of the Church— and the proof is in the healing power of the Eucharist and the adoration chapel. It was amazing sharing and talking with my birth mother, Mary. She makes me feel special and so loved, and I'm glad that she has received healing, too, from us being able to meet and be reconciled. It's so interesting to hear her stories of her family and many generations who were also in the Church.

April 4, 2017

Was excited to sit in the adoration chapel today. Found myself sitting (after kneeling for several minutes) and praying. I was thinking that I wasn't feeling as close to Jesus as I have in the past in here. My mind kept wandering . . . I found myself staring at the beautiful stained glass windows around me. My mind began wondering what I would write about, thinking I might not have too much to write, and then I thought, *That's all right.* And then, just as I was meditating on that, I heard Jesus speaking truth to me. He reminded me that he just loves me, not because of anything I have to do and how I love him, not because of anything he does. Our relationships with other people in this world are sometimes based on what we can get out of them, and he asked me, "How would it make you feel if someone only spent time with you if they got something out of it?" My eyes filled with tears; Jesus loves us unconditionally whether we have something specific to offer him or not. So amazing.

July 31, 2022

Father God, thank you for opening my eyes and getting my attention. I hear you say that I'm seeing it wrong, that the enemy knows my weakness and you, God, are letting him use it to expose me. He thinks he's won because he continues to cause the hurt and throw salt on the old wounds, but I hear you say, Father, that he's using my old hurts and those old memories to try and keep me stuck. I hear you say, "But I am here to expose him and expose his lies. You are moving beyond all this. Yes, it's scary and I know you're scared—you're scared about the next time you'll get your feelings hurt. But I want and need you to realize the hard truth that I'm not ever going to hurt you; I'm not ever going to leave you or forsake you. Even if it was just you and me, I would be more than enough to carry you through any storm! You will never be alone, unloved, or forgotten! Trust me. Look to me all the time. Everyone else in your life will sometimes disappoint you, hurt you, and leave you feeling lonely and empty. Most of the time, they are not doing these things on purpose! They are mere mortals like you! Abide closer to me, and the blanket of comfort I protect you with you will feel more. When Satan is trying to prick you, it will be less sharp, like a dull pain. The pain and sorrow you feel on this earth are temporary!

"Every day, I want you to remind yourself of the GIFT of that day because today you woke up and you get to demonstrate your love for me by how much time you spend with me. By not letting that person's careless words provoke an argument because you are moving past these worldly things. You are in a battle for your soul and the souls of all those you come into contact with each day. They will walk away from you saying either she had peace, she should have been stressed out by this or that, or she was holding her peace. I need them to see me in you.

"I need you to read and meditate on my Word day and night so the schemes of the devil will not completely destroy your peace. It's okay! I'm always here, even when you can't feel me, and you have the opportunity to love me more, to trust me more, to rely on me more. My daughter, never take my love and graces and my protection for granted. Remember my promises! Remember that the sacraments, when utilized with great reverence, will continue to heal and strengthen you!

"You are still on the right path! Do not worry! Every time you worry, you are not seeing me or trusting what I say is true. Just because you're hurting, just because you fight feelings of depression, just because you might have many struggles in a day, you can still say, 'Jesus I trust in you, Jesus I love you,' and as hard as it is, you can trust me. I've told you before, nothing happens to you that I have not permitted. Through the hurt, the depression, and the loneliness is where you really get close to me. This is when I'm protecting you the most. Always trust me, always remember how much I love you, and we will be together soon! Finish the race you are running—you are getting closer! Encourage others as much as possible and share with others; these promises that are for all my dear children. I love you."

Father God, thank you for never giving up on me and for never letting go of my hand. Thank you for reminding me of your great promises and love today! Oh, how I long to please you and share the Good News with others who are still wounded and striving for Heaven! I love you more than anything! Thank you, Jesus.

August 3, 2022

As I lay prostrate alone in the adoration chapel, the Lord gave me my answer, as hard as it was to hear it, but after writing this, he infused me with peace and graces. "I hear what you're telling me, Lord, but as you're telling me, I'm so upset. I find myself crying hysterically because I know the crosses you're asking me to carry," and I say in my loudest, sobbing voice, "You know I'm not this strong! You KNOW I'm not this strong!" I'm upset because I'm so tired and I know you're asking me to keep carrying these crosses.

I then heard you say (very gently with love and tenderness), "Is it harder than what I had to do?" And then I saw you on the cross, and I immediately started apologizing profusely to you, my Lord. "I'm so sorry, of course it's not, Lord; I just think you think I'm stronger than I am. You see me try to keep my peace, and then when I'm attacked, I really try, but I keep failing." Then I heard you telling me to kneel and pray when this happens, and that the most important thing is that I hold my peace. I heard you say, "Go to confession early in the morning tomorrow and then it will be done [what you are doing for me]. Daughter, I love you and your heart for all the sinners and your desire to show them the truth. Be at peace; I'm in control."

I couldn't believe I was getting all this private time, as I lay under the Most Holy Eucharist, and then, all of a sudden, I felt I was at a precipice. If I reached out, I could feel the stone wall in front of me, like the woman who reached out and touched your robe—and when I touched it, I felt you say in my heart, "My daughter, your faith has also healed you."

I couldn't believe it, but I knew it was you. As I rose to my knees with my hands reaching up as close as I could get to you, I said, "I believe! I know it's you; I know you're here," and then fell back in silence in awe of your presence. Once I'm calm, I smile as I imagine that I again looked like an adult child having a temper tantrum. And I chuckled as I asked the Lord, "Does anyone else come in here and have a temper tantrum like this, Lord?

And without a pause I see him smile and say, "Yes."

And I say, "Of course they do, Lord, of course they do! Thank you, dear Lord, for having mercy on my poor soul. Thank you for loving me so much as I struggle with these crosses. Your mercy endures forever."

As I sit and have a private conversation with the Lord, I'm reminded of two attacks by the enemy. I ask him, "Why, Lord, why do the attacks get stronger as I get closer to you?" At first I couldn't hear him, so I quieted my mind even more. Then I heard, "Because the closer you get to me, the bigger the threat you are to him. The closer you are to me, the more souls you will help save." I immediately understood, and it's worth it all; Lord, you are worth it all, and saving one soul is worth all the suffering!

September 6, 2022

Lord, I hear you say, "When your spirits are more lifted, you are getting a false sense of security, and this is dangerous. This is why when you're struggling in life, when depression is strong or the anxiety is strong, you automatically seek me more; you pray more. You need to remember to seek me equally each day, especially on the good days when you may feel like you're soaring and don't need as much help. Whether intentional or not, you need to remember where you have fallen, my daughter. How it pained me to see you turn away from me when I was there trying to warn you out of my love for you. Out of my love for all my people, I tell them to listen to MY voice and to turn from their wicked ways. I am their Heavenly Father and don't want them to get a false sense of security, thinking that because they do this or that they aren't just two choices away from the danger zone. Remember from where you have come and the pit you had to climb out of. It pained me so much, daughter, to see you have to through that, and I don't want my children to suffer like that unnecessarily. Stay humble above all else. Keep your eyes on me; you've come so far in letting go of all the world's opinions and in no longer caring what the world says about you. The only opinion you need to care about is mine.

"Remember, I will never leave you or forsake you, but do not get too comfortable. There are reasons I've told you to attend daily Mass or adoration, and you have limited information. But rest in the information I have given you and the truths that I have allowed you to see! I am enough for you! And when I'm enough for you, you are in a good place, but you are only two steps away from making seemingly innocent choices that could have huge consequences. You know what I have asked you to do and set before you.

"Do not be afraid, daughter! I need you to tell others how much I love them and that they are also just two steps away from falling. Although you fell, you chose to turn from your wicked ways and to seek me with all your heart and soul, like I aways knew you would. But you should always be aware of the danger zone that lurks. You thought you could get close before and keep yourself from falling. You had a false sense of security from the world, and I won't let that happen again. Warn others of the dangers of being lukewarm and what can happen. When you're lukewarm, you are susceptible to the traps of the enemy. Do not let your guard down; do not stop praying; do not stop preparing. Live each day as if it is your last, because then, if it is your last day, if it is your last minute, you will see me, because you chose that day, that minute, to seek my face, to seek my truths. Keep going, daughter, you are on the right path, and I love you!"

September 20, 2022

Lord, I hear you say that we can choose to abide in you each day, each minute. Every thought, every action, every response, and every decision of this day. "You choose to abide in me as I abide in you! Satan comes to steal, kill, and destroy. He comes to steal your joy, to destroy your life, and to kill your spirit. Don't let him steal anything from you ever again! You are mine, daughter! Abide in me as I abide in you!"

Thank you, dear Lord, I am not worthy!

October 18, 2022, Adoration chapel at St. Thomas Moore

"The Lord is just in all his ways and holy in all his works. The Lord is near to all who call upon him, to all who call upon him in truth" (Psalm 145). Heavenly Father, what an effort it took for me to arrive at this adoration chapel today. When I arrived and found someone to be speaking out loud, I felt my spirit get irritated, so I started praying for that person so as to not fault them and then went on praying for other things. Eventually I realized I had been unaware of everyone else in the room for a while, and it was so quiet you could hear a pin drop. I had been so enveloped in your love that I had been unaware of my surroundings for a time. Thank you that we can come adore you, Lord, in the Most Holy Eucharist. I love you so much! I'm so blessed to know you, my Lord! Keep my children safe, please.

October 23, 2022, Adoration chapel at Our Lady of Lourdes

"More tortuous than all else is the human heart, beyond remedy; who can understand it? I, the Lord, alone probe the mind and test the heart, to reward everyone according to his ways, according to the merit of his deeds" (Jeremiah 17:9-10). Father, so much peace comes from knowing who you are! I am nothing! I only must rely on and trust in you fully, and you count my steps, you protect me from myself and from others! If humans could fathom just a little bit of your greatness and who you are, they would truly be set free! Jesus, please make sure I stay little. The only good that comes from me comes from my God! He is everything. I am nothing. I have already won the most important race I will ever run (landing at my Father's feet). I stay here patiently and wait for my next cause. No love compares to that of you, God!

October 24, 2022, Adoration chapel at Our Lady of Loreto

Ephesians 5:1 "Behave like God as his very dear children" (Ephesians 5:1). Father God, I still can't believe all you have saved me from. I'm so not worthy and it has humbled me to my core. The love and trust I have for you grows each day. When you lead me to pray with a dying soul in the privacy of your heart, I disappear, and it becomes you and them. The love they feel from you saves them so often, I believe, and when they pass, I see on their face the peace, Father! Oh, how you love your sons and daughters! Jesus, help me stay close to you always. Help me to serve others better and to make all my amends before my last breath. Jesus, I trust in you!

October 28, 2022, Mass and confession at the Cathedral

"You have entrusted me with a mission, Lord, and you invite me to take responsibility by sharing in your infinite love. At the same time, everything also depends on my response. I must be conscious of the greatness of the mission entrusted to me, which is nothing less than Jesus' mission. *As the Father has sent me, so I send you.*"[15] Father God, I am not worthy to fasten your sandals, let alone proclaim the Gospel to anyone. My only response is to keep with you as your humble, lowly servant, a frequent sinner in love. Please help me with your grace to be worthy of whatever you ask of me. I love you so much. Please help me to overcome my biggest hurdles so I may be of more use to you Father. Jesus, I love you the most. Please show me your face in the exact instances where I need to overcome. Jesus, I trust you.

---

15 *Magnificat* Meditation of the Day, October 28, 2022, page 384.

October 30, 2022, Mass and Confession at St. Mary's

"Many are the trials of the just man but from them all the Lord will rescue him. He will keep guard over his bones, not one of his bones shall be broken. Evil brings death to the wicked; those who hate the good are doomed. The Lord ransoms the souls of his servants. Those who hide in him shall not be condemned" (Psalm 34:19-22). Father God, help me as I continue to struggle. Help me to remember I was once very far from you, my God. Keep me in humility and raise up those needing encouragement. I long to feel your presence and your grace when you feel so far away from me. But I know your promises are true, you are ALWAYS with me, just because I can't feel you, doesn't mean you're not there. Please help me to survive on mere crumbs alone and to be joyful and still praise you. Jesus, stay close to me please.

November 10, 2022, Adoration chapel at Our Lady of Loreto

"Realize, O Christian, your dignity. Once made a partaker of divine nature, do not return to your former baseness by a life unworthy of that dignity. Remember whose head it is and whose body of which you constitute a member. Recall how you had been wrested from the power of darkness and brought into the Kingdom of God" (Colossians 1:13). Father God, How could I ever forget where I have fallen, and thank you, Father, for guiding me on my way back home to you with much more stability being the Most Holy Eucharist and Sacraments. Jesus, I love you! Never let go of my hand!!

November 22, 2022, Basilica of the National Shrine of Mary Queen of the Universe

"Let all the people join to raise, their sweetest songs of love and praise. The solemn festal crowd combines while in the heav'ns this virgin shines, this virgin, resolute and strong, stayed free for Christ her whole life long. She spent her life in praise and prayer and joins the saints in glory fair."[16] Father God, thank you for leading me today to the Basilica of the National Shrine of Mary Queen of the Universe. It helped me so much to receive the Sacrament of Reconciliation and be able to pray in front of the Blessed Sacrament. Thank you for all your holy priests, Father, and please be with and help the ones who are struggling! Seeing and touching Jesus, Mama, and St. Joseph warmed my heart so much. How I long to come home to you all. I need your strength to get through each day here, sometimes each minute. I love you more than anything. Please continue to protect my family!

16 *Magnificat* Hymn, November 22, 2022, page 322.

9 781961 757196